PRAISE FOR CATHY C. BONCZEK AND *THE SIMPLE MAGIC OF EXECUTIVE COMMUNICATION*

"Cathy's work with KKR over the past 15+ years has been based on a simple principle—the power of connection. Her ability to cut through the noise to develop impactful communication strategies has proven invaluable to many of us at KKR, including me. I've seen firsthand how her approach can help transform good communicators into exceptional ones, and she does so with great empathy, warmth, and clarity each step of the way."

—SCOTT NUTTALL

Co-Chief Executive Officer, KKR

"At KKR, one of our guiding values is the importance of 'like and trust,' which often begins with authentic communication that helps cultivate better connections. Whether advising a rising star or seasoned executive, Cathy is extraordinarily talented in empowering leaders to effectively engage with their audience through practical advice and actionable feedback. This book is essential reading for any executive looking to harness the 'simple magic' of communication to make a lasting impact in their organizations and beyond."

—JOSEPH BAE

Co-Chief Executive Officer, KKR

"Whenever a leader is facing a high-profile, high-stakes presentation situation, I call Cathy. She is an astute observer of communication style and provides valuable insight and actionable tools for communication mastery. If you are a leader seeking to improve your presentation, communication, and/or influencing skills, you should have Cathy on speed dial."

—JOAN LAVIN

Former Chief Talent Officer, KKR; Executive Coach and Talent Management Advisor

"Cathy Bonczek understands the power of connecting to, communicating, and engaging with clients, coworkers, and anyone else. Her insights have helped me and can help you be a more effective communicator, leader, and colleague."

—KEN MEHLMAN

Partner, KKR; Campaign Manager, Bush-Cheney 2004; 62nd Chairman of the RNC

"Cathy's approach elevated our team's ability to communicate with clarity, confidence, and authenticity—giving us the tools to tell our story, in our voice. Her blend of warmth and directness made her not only a trusted coach, but a true partner in helping us lead with presence and purpose."

—JULIE SOLOMON

Partner, Co-Head of Real Estate, Ares Management

"Working with Cathy over the years has been one of the most valuable investments our team has made. In a high-performance, client-facing environment, great communication isn't optional—it's essential. Whether we're trying to win business, build trust with clients, or lead a team, the ability to communicate with clarity, confidence, and authenticity is the difference between being good and being great.

"That's where Cathy shines. Her ability to provide guidance that is incisive, pertinent, and immediately actionable—especially for senior professionals who value efficiency—distinguishes her. She's an indispensable extension of our team, and her impact cannot be overstated."

—ANTHONY PAWLOWSKI

Partner, Ares Management

"Cathy has been an exceptional coach, a trusted advisor, and a wonderful friend to me and well over a hundred of my colleagues over the past decade. Regardless of corporate title, industry tenure, or speaking level, Cathy delivers significant value to our professionals across the globe by helping them speak with greater passion, purpose, and punchiness. Thank you very much, Cathy, for your incredible partnership."

—RYAN BERRY

Partner, Chief Marketing and Strategy Officer, Ares Management

"Effective communication is a prerequisite for success. Cathy helps to elevate an executive's message, so that he or she can have a bigger impact on their most important constituents."

—HENRY MCVEY

Head of Global Macro & Asset Allocation and Firmwide Market Risk, CIO of the KKR Balance Sheet, and Co-Head of KKR's Strategic Partnership Initiative, KKR

"Cathy has been an outstanding partner to Arctos, helping us elevate the way we communicate and present with confidence. Her coaching has not only strengthened each of us as individuals but also enhanced how we collaborate and deliver as a team. Cathy's expertise and practical guidance have made a lasting impact."

—GREGORY C. BAECHER

Partner, Arctos Partners

"Coach Cathy has been instrumental in my career, helping me find clarity and confidence in both what I say and how I carry myself as a leader. She's not just a coach, but a trusted guide in all things communication and professional growth."

—ELEANOR MCENANEY

Director, Global Impact, KKR

"I've found myself repeatedly thinking back to my notes from our sessions and applying them in real time to interactions with others (and not just at work!). I've not only improved in my ability to speak with conviction and impact, but feel like my confidence has increased tenfold in meetings that I previously would have felt surges of anxiety throughout in anticipation of having to speak . . .

"I found Cathy's style of directness and relatability incredibly impactful—it created a comfortable space for us to experiment with our presentation approach and learn from mistakes without fear of judgment. I feel so fortunate to have gotten the opportunity to be part of this program."

—EMILY RICHNER

Manager, Human Capital Business Partner, KKR

THE SIMPLE MAGIC OF EXECUTIVE COMMUNICATION

THE SIMPLE MAGIC OF EXECUTIVE COMMUNICATION

FORGET PERFECTION.
COMMUNICATION THAT CHANGES EVERYTHING
BEGINS WITH CONNECTION.

CATHY C. BONCZEK

Forbes | Books

Published by Forbes Books, Charleston, South Carolina.
An imprint of Advantage Media Group.

Printed in the United States of America.

10 9 8 7 6 5 4 3 2 1

ISBN: 979-8-88750-703-3 (Hardcover)
ISBN: 979-8-88750-704-0 (eBook)

Library of Congress Control Number: 2026902184

Cover design by Sullivan (SULLIVANNYC.com).
Layout design by Lance Buckley.

02-07-2026 3:18

To John, Peter, and Jamie,

Your unwavering love, support, and belief in me have been the foundation of every step I've taken. This book is as much yours as it is mine. Thank you for your patience and encouragement, and for always showing me what truly matters in life. I am forever grateful for the strength and inspiration you give me every day.

To my clients, your trust, brilliance, and dedication continually inspire me. This book is dedicated to all of you, for reminding me of the power of transformation and for allowing me to be part of your journey.

With heartfelt gratitude.

CONTENTS

ACKNOWLEDGMENTS

I would like to extend my deepest gratitude to the following individuals and organizations whose contributions and support were essential in bringing this book to life:

To the CCB team: Tahra Millan, Rene Hampton, and Lisa DeCamella: Words can hardly express how deeply grateful I am for each of you. Your dedication, copious talents, and shared vision have been the driving force behind everything we've achieved. You consistently go above and beyond, and your commitment to excellence inspires me every day. Working with such a remarkable team has been one of the greatest privileges of this journey, and I am beyond thankful for your support, passion, and belief in what we do together. You make the impossible feel possible, and this book would not have been possible without you.

To Peter Rogen and Neil Flett—communicators extraordinaire. I can't thank you enough for what you put in motion and into the world. To the extended Rogen family: What fun it was to start this journey with you!

To my extended family and friends:

First, Mom and Dad, who are no longer with me, but remain my examples of integrity, intelligence, curiosity, and unconditional love. No better people. To my sister, Caryn, who always challenges and pushes me with relentless honesty and valuable insights: I love you more than you know. In remembrance of my "second mother," Janet Sarno: Thank you for teaching me to act with abandon, love wildly, and write like my life depended on it. Special love to Celeste, the Big C, who gets me through it all.

Thanks, too, to my Westhill friends and Mr. Hobby's Northstar Players (who first gave me a stage), the Sweet Briar Five, my Ladies of the Book, my Kappa sisters, and the Orchid Girls—friends for life that make my world so much richer.

To Cornell University, my beloved alma mater, for helping make me the English-major-who-got-a-job out of college, and for giving me the world.

Thank you to Meghan Stevenson, for getting me to dream bigger.

Light and beauty to Drew Lamm, the muse, who gives me poetry, words, and a new perspective every week.

Thank you to Elizabeth Kennedy for your meticulous editing, guidance, and unwavering commitment to enhancing the manuscript. Your expertise has helped shape this book into something I am proud to share.

To my collaborator-in-chief, Wilene Dunn, whose talents and warmth got me through all the chapters—with prayers and a song.

Thank you to Dale DeSmet and Sean Essex of TRACOM, for allowing me to include the Social Style Model™ in this book and for your contributions to this work. It has had a profound impact on my life and work.

Finally, to Forbes Books for giving me the incredible opportunity to join their group of distinguished authors. It is an honor to be a part of the team.

Your collective dedication, support, and expertise have made this book a reality, and I am forever grateful for each of you.

FOREWORD

By Pete Stavros
Co-Head of Global Private Equity at KKR

You're about to read a book filled with wisdom on how to communicate and connect in an authentic way that will help your messages land more clearly and memorably than ever before. I only wish I'd had the benefit of Cathy's advice much earlier.

I've always been afraid of public speaking. Not "throw-up" afraid, but close. Part of that came from my dad, who grew up terrified of the idea due to a stutter and his limited formal education. He used to say, "I'd rather be dead than speak in front of a crowd." I absorbed that fear.

For years, I managed to avoid public speaking altogether. That changed in ninth grade, when I had to give a short talk about a book of my choosing. I picked the autobiography of Jim McMahon, the quarterback for the 1986 Chicago Bears Super Bowl team. I never thought about what my classmates or my teacher might actually want to hear; I just liked the Bears. I wrote out the speech word-for-word, read it straight from the page, never looked up, and delivered something very flat. I knew it was bad before I sat down.

The only feedback I got was a C grade, which told me nothing about how to improve and further reinforced that I should just keep avoiding public speaking. In college I stuck with chemistry and math, fields where there was little risk of standing in front of a group. But eventually, like most people, I couldn't avoid it forever.

At business school, the format was eighty students in a single classroom discussion. The thought of participating terrified me. I was so nervous that, the summer before, I enrolled in Toastmasters. It helped, but only a little. I still found myself so preoccupied with what I might say next that I wasn't actually listening. The first time I spoke up in class, I repeated something someone else had just said. My professor stopped me: "Pete, Brendan made that exact point one minute ago. Try to stay present."

I came to believe that public speaking was a gift, something some people were lucky to have, and that I wasn't one of the lucky ones.

That changed when I began working with Cathy Bonczek more than fifteen years ago. Methodically, she taught me not just how to give a talk, but how to communicate. She helped me think about what I wanted to say, who my audience was, and why they should care.

She trained me to stop using dense slides as a crutch and instead keep things simple, sometimes even a single image, so the audience would stay focused on my message. She reminded me that if I avoided eye contact, I was also avoiding connection. And she showed me that authenticity isn't something you add on at the end; it's something you bring with you from the very start.

Cathy's coaching has carried me through some of the most demanding situations of my career: a talk on the main stage at TED, interviews on *60 Minutes* and *CBS Sunday Morning*, even small group conversations where the outcome really mattered. Each time, her advice was the same: Be yourself, connect with your audience, keep in mind why your material matters to them, and know the content so well that you can stay in the moment. Oh, and if you can bear it, record yourself preparing and watch it back. No one will catch lapses in presence, eye contact, or authenticity better than you will, and seeing it for yourself makes the lesson stick in a way nothing else does.

I once ran into Cathy just after she had finished a session with one of the most eloquent and polished business leaders I know. I remember thinking, *That person uses a coach?* Over time, I've come to realize that nearly all accomplished communicators do. The ability to speak and connect effectively isn't a gift; it's a skill. And like any skill, it *can* be learned.

That's why this book matters. In these pages, Cathy distills decades of experience into practical, memorable lessons that anyone can apply. If you take the time to read and internalize her wisdom, the greatest benefit won't be to you—it will be to your audience, and to the impact you're trying to make in the world.

INTRODUCTION

The Simple Magic of Executive Communication has been my labor of love for more than thirty years. As a coach to senior executives around the world, I've learned that communication is so much more than just sharing information; it is a masterful art of connection, trust, confidence, and inspiring others to action.

This book is my gift to you, and I hope that the insights and tools that I have gathered over decades will prove useful to you as you navigate your career.

People often ask me how I became a communications consultant, and I say, "I asked the universe for the job." I then tell them how, at the end of a one-year break from my then career, a headhunter called to ask, "When are you coming back? I have several banks that want to hire you."

I told her, "I don't think I'm going back to banking. I've gotten out!"

She laughed and asked, "What do you want to do next?"

I said, "I just know that I want to help people through communication, and I want it to be international."

She said, "Well, I happen to have this one search on my desk for an international communications company. I'm sending you to the interview!"

That's how I found Rogen International (eventually known as rogenSi) and changed careers. And what an adventure it's been since then.

I have been fortunate to work with leaders across industries as they have navigated complex global markets and led their teams through transformative changes.

Through these experiences, I've come to appreciate how nuanced communication can be; every message resonates differently because of the individual who is saying it out loud.

I've also learned that leaders don't often receive the feedback they need in order to improve. Subordinates are worried about offending or seeming too critical. Yet, an honest assessment of your strengths and your development opportunities is critical to mastering a strong voice.

Every speaker has a choice in how much they want to practice, how much they want to connect, and how much they want to inspire. The bottom line is this: Communication is a powerful tool, and it can be mastered whether you were born with innate ability or not.

I have always felt that the tools one uses are simple, but the results are often magical. I benefited from starting my communication career at Rogen International (later rogenSi).

The rogenSi Origin Story

The rogenSi story began in 1968 when a New York off-Broadway actor, Peter Rogen, was asked to improve the executive presentation skills of the executives at global advertising giant Grey. He did so by creating a three-day workshop that involved a unique combination of communication and acting skills, exercises, and practice. The rogenSi program worked extraordinarily well, and Peter had laid the foundations for a business that would go on to help thousands of individuals and organizations in more than one hundred countries achieve exceptional performance.

In 1987, one of rogenSi's participants was Neil Flett, a public relations man and journalist who took a license for the presentation skills program in Australia and, over the next six years, took on partners and grew rogenSi in other parts of the world, including Asia, New Zealand, Canada, the United States, and London. With that growth came an expansion beyond presentation skills to sales, influencing, negotiation, facilitation, and leadership skills, plus a host of other training and consulting solutions tailored specifically to help organizations win. The rogenSi business was becoming renowned for having practical and proven programs delivered by world-class facilitators that gave organizations the knowledge and skills required to help them win.[1] Peter and Neil created methodologies and programs that bolstered the skills of professionals around the world. I joined a charismatic group in New York City, trained in Sydney at the onset, and became a communications consultant. As others came and went, regardless of when they joined the firm, it was always apparent that a Rogen-trained consultant was a special breed.

Many of these colleagues are now leading their own communications businesses, evidence of the pivotal role Rogen played in shaping the field of executive communication and transforming countless careers. Their contributions have left an indelible mark, inspiring future generations to adopt and elevate their communication practices.

This book is designed for executives, leaders, and professionals who aspire to move into a space where authenticity, emotional intelligence, and purposeful impact intersect. Whether you are preparing for a board meeting, a team presentation, or a casual conversation, the principles outlined in these pages will help you elevate your message and engage your audience in ways that create lasting influence.

---

1 "rogenSi is now part of ttec," ttec, https://www.ttec.com/rogensi-is-now-part-of-ttec.

I believe that true leadership is rooted in authenticity. It's not about perfection; it's about connection. It's important for you, as a leader and a communicator, to be attentive, present, and aligned with your message and values. The simple magic of communication lies in finding your voice, speaking with purpose, and fostering genuine connections that inspire action and drive results.

Throughout this book, we will explore the core elements of executive communication, from understanding your audience and honing your message to mastering delivery techniques that ensure your voice resonates. By the end, you will have the tools to confidently navigate many communication challenges with poise, clarity, and authenticity. Of course, there is no substitute for in-person coaching and the immediate feedback that it provides, but these foundational tools are essential to your mastery.

People who inspire others are not just good leaders; they are good communicators. They motivate others through their messages, their values, their commitment, and their clarity. I invite you to step into this journey with me, discover the transformative power of executive communication, and unlock your ability to create authentic impact every time you speak.

PART 1

GETTING READY TO STEP INTO THE SPOTLIGHT

1

PURSUING THE PERFECT PITCH

"I don't have perfect pitch, but I have relative pitch. I'm glad I don't have perfect pitch because perfect pitch can drive you crazy."

—BILLY ECKSTINE

Throughout my life, I've been captivated by the power of words—the way they can inspire, persuade, and connect us. I graduated from Cornell University with an English degree and the ability to speak fluent French, which, as you can imagine, made me highly employable. From crafting essays to coaching leaders in the art of communication, I've come to realize that true mastery goes beyond what we say; it's about how we make others feel heard and understood.

I began my work on Wall Street, or just below, on Broadway, working for a French shipping firm called Worms. It was affiliated with Banque Worms, and, for some reason, no one liked my suggestion that we should call ourselves "Worms in the Big Apple."

I started as an executive assistant and was quickly promoted to Suez Canal specialist. My job was to help shipowners navigate the Suez Canal from end to end, pulling the correct draught in the waters and paying the appropriate fees at both ends of the canal.

There was just one hitch. Neither the shipowners nor the port officials would work with a young woman. Since most of the communication was done by telex, I was Mr. Cathy for two years.

Two years later, I came in one day, and my boss told me he had entered me into the Miss Maritime Beauty Contest. His explanation was that he thought I would win hands down.

I left Worms and decided to go find a job where the women were. And in my youth and naivete, I walked into a bank.

The bank was Irving Trust, and the man who interviewed me said he did so because I was fluent in French. The job didn't require fluency in French; he just liked French.

When they hired me to be a personal banker, he said, "We can teach you how to be a banker, but we can't teach you how to be great with people. You are great with people, and that's what we need."

And that's how my journey to being a communications coach began.

It's my hope to challenge the notion of perfection in business presentations and encourage you to create effective and enjoyable communications. I know these skills can be learned. It doesn't have to be just one of those things you were born with. I don't want you wasting time striving for flawless delivery because that can be counterproductive. Focusing on the message and audience connection leads to more impactful presentations. My intention is that you will feel empowered to prioritize genuine engagement over perceived perfection.

The Right Note

I've never met a client who started an engagement with, "I'd like to be average in my communication skills."

More often, my clients are looking to become "perfect" presenters: the kind of speakers who look as if they were born with the skill to mesmerize and enchant audiences.

I liken this to the concept of perfect pitch in music. People who sing often say they would like to have perfect pitch. According to the University of Chicago, "Perfect pitch refers to a person's ability to identify any musical note by name after hearing it, without reference to other notes. Perfect pitch—also known more technically as absolute pitch—can also refer to the ability that some singers have to sing a given note on cue."[2]

Perfect pitch is a rare talent that one in ten thousand people might possess. Most musicians have relative pitch: the ability to recognize notes in relation to each other.

I believed that my sister, Caryn, had perfect pitch. As a family, we used to sit around the piano and sing. Caryn was a first soprano. Mom was an alto and could harmonize with any tune. Dad and I were usually off pitch. Anything that Dad did, we loved, so we found it endearing that he would get approximately close to the right tune. However, when I would sing, Caryn would say, "You're off-key" or "That's not the right note."

Yet, I always thought of myself as a singer. Being off-key didn't dissuade me from the idea that I should be making music. When I was in high school and started babysitting, I immediately used my earned money to engage a voice teacher. I learned relative pitch, how to breathe properly, and how to harmonize with other voices—all great skills for singing, but also for communicating!

My sister and I enjoyed many years of singing together in different choirs, including St. Patrick's Cathedral Choir in New York City. The takeaway is that, with proper training—and a stubborn streak—you can get really good at finding your right note.

---

2 Max Witynski, "Perfect Pitch, Explained," *UChicago News*, https://news.uchicago.edu/explainer/what-is-perfect-pitch.

I have built a career around helping people bridge that gap: between knowing they are meant to be saying important things to important people but not feeling that they are on pitch—just yet. With that in mind, let's talk about how the pursuit of perfection can get in the way of being great.

In business, presenters often waste a lot of time and energy in the pursuit of "perfection"—getting the slides and materials exactly right before they focus on the overall message. They aspire to give a flawless delivery that is error-free. That's like focusing only on the notes of a song and not thinking about the story or the overall emotion or enjoyment the song can provide.

Here's how it often manifests: You are asked to present on a topic to either an internal or external audience. It is high stakes, and many bosses will be in the audience. You have three weeks until the event. You try to find out if anyone in the firm has ever talked about this subject before, and if they have, you take their old PowerPoint and start from there. Or, you may be the first person to speak on this topic, in which case, you begin to research everything and anything you can about it.

You amass information and statistics and facts in order to be the most knowledgeable person in the room on the subject. But you start to get a niggling fear that you are an imposter because you don't have total knowledge.

You spend nearly two weeks collecting data, and in the final week, you focus on the PowerPoint deck. You spend hours adding words and charts to the pages. You may even have to submit the deck to the legal and/or compliance team for final edits.

When there is only a day or two left before the event, you realize that you need to rehearse, so you say the presentation out loud and flip through the pages. More often than not, you will stop to correct a typo or write a speaking note on the deck.

This is a surefire way to enter the room, or go onto the stage, feeling a bit unrehearsed, unsteady, and embarrassed in advance.

You have fallen into the trap that most presenters do, which is measuring your success by getting to the last page of the deck. And you have bought into the myth of perfect presentations, which is

1. that they exist, and
2. that they are to be desired.

What you've gained in this process is a lot of anxiety, a lot of wasted time, and a presentation that does not reflect anything about who you are as a person.

By focusing your efforts on "getting it right," "making it perfect," and "being the expert," you have lost sight of the most important goal: connecting with your audience. If you had taken the time to think about how to make the main message clear and the engagement robust, you would have opted for a simpler delivery and shown up as your authentic, brilliant self: a much-preferred outcome.

Let's revisit the concept of relative pitch. We know it's possible to still make beautiful music without perfect pitch.

To make this relevant to our business presentations, relative pitch is the idea that the core messages need to be delivered in a conversational manner, in the way that best suits your audience and who you are. Harmony comes from paying attention to the people you are singing with, so you need to learn how to pause, listen, read the room, adjust your message, and delve into any reactions.

To start to build our relative pitch, or harmony, let's ask the following questions:

- How do you lean into your imperfections so that your audience will like and trust you?

- How should you interact with your audience? Why is rapport so highly sought after?
- Would you rather sit through a presentation during which the presenter asks you to speak, react, and offer opinions but also makes you laugh? Or would you prefer someone to deliver twenty to thirty pages of content *at* you? Which presenter would you like to ask to lunch? Which presenter would you invite to the next brainstorming session?

The bottom line is this: We measure success in communications not by the flawlessness of the delivery but by the substance of the discourse and the engagement of the audience.

By accepting the power of relative pitch—and releasing the restraints of perfect pitch—you will find your own voice, be more empowered, and deliver a more engaging presentation.

A shift from perfectionism to meaningful communication, from perfect pitch to relative pitch, is the goal.

When I decided to leave the bank I was then working at, Bank of Boston, and return to New York City, things had taken a turn at work that made it easier to leave. I had a challenging boss who had just given a promotion to his rumored lover, and I was discouraged by what was being handled and what was being hidden.

I resigned and called my boss's boss and asked him to join me for coffee. He agreed. When we met, he started the conversation by saying, "What can I do to convince you to stay?" He was new in his role and had been impressed by my reputation and accomplishments.

I told him that I could not be persuaded, nor could I leave in good conscience without speaking truth. I pulled out an agenda and started by asking him to simply listen and to understand that there might be a little emotion underpinning my viewpoint. He laughed and said he would be sure to factor that in.

We had a fulsome discussion about the department, the region, and the projects that were outstanding. I was honest about the positive aspects of each, and I gave him my perspective on the issues I felt were being kept from him. I remember making a plea for him to improve the compensation of the retail team or at least increase the transparency on what could reasonably be expected each year. We talked about the ways to inspire others to stay committed and ways to make sure they felt valued.

I was exhausted by this conversation because brutal honesty takes energy. I didn't feel imperiled; I had already resigned. Yes, offering your unvarnished opinions is an act of vulnerability. He thanked me profusely and said that he'd been aware of some of what we talked about, but not all of it. The perspective was incredibly helpful to him.

This was a moment when I appreciated the power of honest communication. Speaking your opinion has value, whether or not the person you're speaking to agrees with you. I remember his careful attention to all that I said and how much it meant to me to have the opportunity to say it all out loud. Six months later, he called me at my new place of employment to tell me about the changes he had implemented as a result of our conversation.

Whether you're delivering tough feedback, offering a new perspective, or simply seeking to be heard, the courage to speak up is foundational to effective communication. It's not always about getting someone to agree with you—it's about sharing your truth with respect and doing so in a way that invites understanding and growth.

As we move forward in this book, remember that communication is not a one-way street. It's about connection, clarity, and courage. The way you communicate shapes how you show up in the world and how the world perceives you. So, as you consider the conversations that lie ahead, think about this manager's attentiveness and ask yourself, "How can I use my voice, honestly and authentically, to create meaningful change?"

Returning to the concept of perfectionism, it's important to recognize that letting go of perfectionism doesn't mean abandoning quality or purpose in our communication. Instead, it means focusing on the message and the connection we create with our audience rather than obsessing over every detail or striving for flawlessness. So, how do we begin this shift?

The first step is to acknowledge that *perfection is an illusion*—a goal that only serves to heighten anxiety and distance us from what really matters. We must give ourselves permission to *be imperfect*, to embrace the natural flow of conversation, and to trust that our audience wants to engage with *us*—the real, authentic version of ourselves—not some polished, idealized version.

Here's how we begin to *embrace relative pitch*:

1. **Shift your focus from perfection to connection:** Instead of worrying about getting every word right, concentrate on creating a connection with your audience. Ask yourself: *How can I make this message resonate with them?*

2. **Practice being present:** When we focus on perfection, we often become rigid, reciting a rehearsed script. Instead, practice being present—listening to your audience's reactions and adjusting as needed. Allow the conversation to flow, just as musicians adjust their pitch to harmonize with the rest of the band.

3. **Lean into your imperfections:** The things you might see as flaws are often what make you relatable and human.

Embrace them. The audience is not looking for someone flawless—they're looking for someone real, someone who makes them feel heard and understood.

4. **Rehearse to Converse:** Rehearsal isn't just about getting the words right—it's about embodying your message. Practice delivering it in a way that feels comfortable and natural to you. This will help you move away from a mechanical delivery and toward a more engaging, conversational style.

By letting go of the pursuit of perfection, you open the door to more authentic and impactful communication. And that's exactly where we'll start our next chapter—by understanding who you're communicating with and tailoring your approach to make sure that connection happens.

2

EARLY LESSONS AND PLANNING STEPS

"Plans are nothing; planning is everything."

—DWIGHT D. EISENHOWER

In chapter 1, we explored the idea of relative pitch—the concept that, much like musicians adjusting their notes in relation to each other, a communicator must tune their message to their audience and context. Just as you can learn to harmonize with others, effective communicators must adapt and adjust their delivery to ensure their message resonates with those listening.

Now, as we move into chapter 2, we'll dive into practical steps to help you build this relative pitch in your communications. Whether it's understanding your audience, setting clear objectives, or knowing which information to present, these steps are critical for ensuring your message hits the right note. By approaching each conversation, presentation, or meeting with intention, you'll be ready to deliver your message in a way that's both compelling and authentic—just as a musician harmonizes with their ensemble. Remember: This isn't about perfection; it's about finding your own voice and making sure the audience is with you every step of the way.

In my early career days, when I was helping shipowners navigate the Suez Canal and toggling daily between English and French, I learned that having 90 percent of my message being understood was a victory. We were speaking to captains from all over the world and to crews flying under the flags of numerous countries. English was not universal, but we had to convey important facts and information to them to make their travels safe. They had to know what draught they could pull in shallow canal waters and what the expected payments would be (and the expected bribes of cigarette cartons in those days).

In my youth, and with my newly minted English major, I was disdainful of my manager's poor language skills in English. I watched him connect with prospects and clients and then hand over nearly illiterate reports of the meetings. He often expected me to transcribe the notes. At first, I tried to edit them and turn them into some semblance of a narrative. Then I decided that was too time-consuming and just typed them up verbatim.

The assistant manager told me that I was out of line and that I should continue to turn the notes into proper meeting minutes. In response, I handed her the notes from that day's meetings and said, "You take these home and edit them. Then tomorrow, you can tell me how to do it better."

The next day, she came in, handed the reports back to me, and said, "Just type down exactly what he's written; don't bother trying to make them make sense!"

That was my first corporate experience with letting go of perfectionism and realizing that the words on the page were only a part of the story.

I became a "student" again when I joined Irving Trust. My tiny class of five personal bankers learned all the details about accounts and how to open them. There was no time spent on how to interact with customers. That was left for us to figure out.

I was assigned to the Park Avenue branch (245 Park Avenue) and had to speak to dozens of existing and potential customers every day. I learned to explain bank rules clearly to many different types of people, how to negotiate fees, how to spot a cross-sale opportunity, and even how to identify a fraud. I was promoted to be one of the lead personal bankers.

I was recruited away by Marine Midland Bank, where I was asked to pioneer a product called Premier Service—an elite banking service for those clients who held higher balances than the average account holder but did not yet qualify for private banking classification.

I was to offer them the kid-glove treatment when they needed banking services. Here, I learned that being good at communication was a premier skill. The role didn't protect me from rude or angry customers, but I gained an appreciation for the importance of listening before reacting, and of not taking someone else's anger personally.

I was promoted to branch manager and relocated to the Upper East Side. My clients were wealthy and sophisticated. The physical branch was small, but I was in charge of the safety of the entire team of ten. I remember learning how to vary my route to work every day so that potential bank robbers wouldn't follow me to figure out our routine.

In the course of my banking career, I experienced a half dozen bank robberies.

I had been educated and prepared for handling bank robberies because that was a part of the business. The money lost wouldn't be the issue; the trauma the act could cause to the bank personnel was the concern. Our training emphasized the importance of becoming keen observers, not just to try to thwart potential harm but also to bear witness when the police arrived later.

Emergency communication is a different skill from everyday communication. Being able to remain calm when someone points a gun at you is part of it; being able to restore a sense of safety to a team is another.

I changed banks two more times, each time being put in charge of larger and larger teams.

At Chemical Bank, I once was able to "*feel*" that something was off. I called my (new) manager and asked if I could get a security guard to protect the branch. He laughed and said, "We don't do that here; what's going on?" I said, "I feel as if we're going to be robbed today." He reiterated that they didn't supply guards.

Thirty minutes later, my branch was robbed. This was the era when I learned to trust my instincts and the nonverbal messages we receive from people around us. Not all communication is verbal.

In fact, it was communication that led to my leaving New York City and moving to Boston. A recruiter approached my desk one day and said, "I've been watching you for a while. The way you interact with clients is amazing. I was asked to come find a branch manager for Bank of Boston, but I want to recommend you as an area manager."

I was single and ambitious, and that sounded good to me!

I joined Bank of Boston as the area manager in charge of a dozen branches and approximately two hundred and fifty people. I was the youngest area manager—and the first female one. This was the phase of my career when I learned even more about leadership communication: how you build trust and inspire others to run their own businesses (for each branch was its own cost center).

I learned that sharing information with my supposed competitors—the other area managers—was better for the bank and better for business; besides, it was more fun.

One tough lesson was realizing that the onslaught of emails, memos, meetings, and emergencies was never going to be tamed. It was up to me to decide to focus my attention and time on the higher-priority communications.

One day, my boss's boss, George, came in and said, "Quick! We need someone to go down to the auditorium and speak to two hundred people about why they would want to work at the bank!"

I jumped up and said, "I'll do it!"

That's how I found myself on stage, talking to a large room of people about the amazing bank and all it could offer.

I received great feedback afterward because I had spoken from the heart and been very enthusiastic, but in truth, I had really just rambled. I got by on style, but I don't know if what I said was truly memorable.

I did get a call later from my boss's boss, who told me his niece had been in the audience and had given me a great review. Thank goodness!

My audiences got bigger as time went on. I moved to one last bank, NatWest Bank, when I got engaged and returned to New York City. I took on an area manager role and was eventually promoted to regional marketing and distribution officer in charge of the borough of Queens.

In this role, I found that it was even more important to understand the needs of an audience. In order to keep the Queens team motivated, there needed to be constant interactions, each one suited to the individual. There was another kind of interaction needed to speak on behalf of the whole borough when I was in the leadership meetings.

I hadn't yet mastered my strong, strident voice. The diplomatic and warm way that had led me to success thus far was not the right "voice" for this bank. I was told that I was too honest and that I smiled too much. My manager said in my review, "You are too nice."

Talk about bad feedback! I wanted to scream, "What about all of the accomplishments? The staff that I've fired and hired to create stronger teams? The borough results, which are great? Do you think that all happened by accident?" But I didn't scream, and in hindsight, I should have fought with him. I took that commentary on the chin and eventually left the bank because I felt unseen and unappreciated.

How lucky for me that happened! It caused me to ask a recruiter to find me something "that helps people through communication, preferably internationally."

That's what led me to Rogen International (as it was called then) and a career as a communications consultant.

That's when I started to help people get ready to deliver great messages. It was soon apparent that a lot of professionals were meeting with clients without doing any preparation whatsoever.

This is a common experience. I like to say that my clients hire brilliant people, then keep them so busy bringing in business that they find themselves running into meeting rooms and conducting meetings without any forethought or rehearsal.

Does this sound familiar to you?

For example, if you come in on a Monday and your manager says, "We have to do a presentation to a prospect on Wednesday!" you and your colleagues might jump to immediate action.

One person will start gathering facts, another will dig out last month's PowerPoint deck, and one will begin typing up a script. Each of them will pick up their phone and cancel any evening plans they had.

Again, sound familiar?

I've heard countless tales of clients jumping into taxis to get to their prospects' offices, with newly minted decks that they peruse on the ride over. There is no time to review the decks and certainly no time to rehearse who's going to say what.

It doesn't have to be this way.

I have since learned that taking a step back and planning to succeed is more effective than just relying on your instincts and in-the-moment skills.

You might argue, if time were expandable and there were days to prepare, I'd be able to prepare for meetings and presentations. It's all the more important to plan, even when time is short. Without thinking through the following categories, you will end up with an unformed and uninformed message.

Without considering the following elements, your message risks being unclear and ungrounded.

Let's walk through the key steps to help get any speaker ready for a meeting or presentation.

Start with the most important part of any communication: To whom are you talking?

Audience Analysis

The starting point is always the audience.

Have you found yourself sidestepping the question of your audience? Maybe your reasoning goes something like this: "The relationship manager knows the person and will tell me what I need to know."

Maybe you rely on titles and roles, using them to make assumptions about what the prospect will be interested in. That's a potentially helpful step, but it's not wholly accurate or reliable. It's a huge advantage to resist being complacent about this step. People will enter the room carrying the psychological baggage of the meeting they just left or a project they left on their desk to meet with you. There are so many variables that can affect a person's readiness to listen.

And so many questions to answer!

To whom are you speaking? Who will be in the room? If there is more than one person in the room, who is the most important person? Who makes the decisions? What is the decision-making process? Who influences that person? Who supports you, your firm, or your idea?

Who is a detractor? What do they actually know versus what do they think they know?

How do they like to get their information? Do they prefer visuals? Data? Numbers and characters on the slides?

Do they trust you or your organization? Have they had positive or negative experiences with others in your field?

What are their values?

Imagine you've invited some guests to your home for a dinner party. You hold up the platter for them to admire, and then you say, "I've seasoned this to *your* taste. Dig in." So it is with great communication. You've taken the time to tailor your words, energy, and visuals to be well suited to your listener.

I recommend making your starting point the SOCIAL STYLE® Model, which we will cover in chapter 3.

After assessing your audience, you need to determine what you want to accomplish.

Set an Objective

During my time at Rogen International, I had the opportunity to work with top-level executives, helping them refine their communication skills to drive business success. These experiences deeply shaped my approach to coaching and communication, giving me a honed perspective on how powerful effective leadership communication can be.

We always asked, "What do you want your audience to think, do, or feel?" Clients would say to me, "I know what my objective is: Get the business! Bring in the money!" That's right, of course, but in the first meeting, a better objective might be to ensure they leave the meeting feeling as if it were time well spent, thinking that you and your firm are the best ones suited to help them—and agreeing to another meeting immediately.

And the next meeting? The objective could be to get the agreement signed or the investment amount secured. These are examples of business objectives.

It's equally important to spend time crafting a personal objective, the one that you won't say out loud to your colleagues but that is critical to your brand. What do you want your audience to think, do, or feel about you? I recommend you choose five powerful words to define yourself and what you want people to learn about you by the end of any encounter.

Do you see yourself as a visionary? As charismatic? As a critical thinker? As the next leader of the firm? As confident, engaging, reliable, insightful, or inspiring?

Choosing your five defining words is a quick way to create a powerful impression and give your audience the right insight about who you are. If you hold these words in your heart and mind, they manifest in how you hold your body and posture. You don't have to say to your audience, "You will find me charismatic, engaging, and inspiring," because they will sense it.

Identify Persuasive Data

Imagine you're in a meeting with a potential client. You've prepared an extensive presentation, filled with facts, figures, and case studies. But halfway through, you notice the client's attention drifting. They've heard enough—they don't need every detail you've collected. What they need is the right information at the right time, and perhaps a little proof to back it up.

> ***What they need is the right information at the right time, and perhaps a little proof to back it up.***

Most business communicators face this challenge. We often gather an overwhelming amount of data, but in reality, our clients and colleagues only need a small fraction of it to be persuaded. The key is identifying that critical piece of information, delivering it with impact, and showing why it matters to them.

Structure the Message

It's all about story! Every great story needs a beginning, a middle, and an end. Your clarity will improve by using outlines to guide you as you write and deliver your message. I'll share an outline that I recommend, and we'll also explore what truly makes a story stand out. Here's a hint: It's not about the facts—it's about the emotions.

Consider Your Visual Aids

In the financial markets, where I coach most of the time, the visual aid of choice is the pitch book or deck, prepared in the ubiquitous PowerPoint presentation. When preparing a communication, we need to think about what visuals will enhance our audience's retention of the information. Also important is the type of visual aid needed to stay on point and keep our attention on the people in the room. There's nothing worse than staring at the top of someone's head while they're reading from a deck.

Run-Through and Rehearsal

When people ask me what it will take to become an amazing communicator, I say, "Rehearsal." That's the best and most effective way to improve your skills. It's important to "fail," either by being too stiff or too silly, in the rehearsal. You use those outer limits to stretch the possibilities of what you can do, and then you choose what demeanor best suits you, your audience, and your topic. What is the difference between a run-through and a rehearsal?

Let's start with the run-through, when you "put your mouth around the words" of the message or presentation. In business, we are often given a message, scripted to perfection, that must be delivered to our clients. It is very hard to deliver someone else's message. It takes some time to say it in a way that you would naturally say it. Translating an important message into your own lexicon is powerful and credible.

A run-through is what actors do when they are first handed a script. They read it out loud to get a sense of the overall storyline; they get an initial feel for the emotional journey and what the most important lines are in the entire piece. They also start to work on the chemistry between the actors/roles.

In business, it's a good idea to think about who will start the presentation and who will follow and craft the transitions between the sections. Why leave it to chance when a fifteen-minute run-through will help you look seamless and unified as a presenting team?

Rehearse to Converse

Why do you need a full-on rehearsal, where you start at the beginning and present until the end?

You rehearse to converse.

When you know the heart of your messages, you can then relax and let those messages come out in a less scripted way. This will be far more fun for you and your audience.

In rehearsal, we also touch on all the delivery skills: eye contact, voice, gestures, posture, and movement. These are the skills that famous actors know how to wield. We in business should be as rehearsed and talented.

It's sobering to realize that most of your impact comes from how you deliver the message, *not what you say.*

- **Seven percent is the words:** This refers to the idea that only 7 percent of the meaning behind a message is conveyed through the literal words used.
- **93 percent is how you do it:** This signifies that the remaining 93 percent of the message is communicated through nonverbal aspects such as facial expressions, gestures, and tone of voice.

This concept is often attributed to psychologist Albert Mehrabian's 7-38-55 rule, which states that 7 percent of communication is conveyed through words, 38 percent through tone of voice, and 55 percent through body language.

These delivery skills are the building blocks of your executive presence, as well. That is why rehearsal is the route to presentation brilliance.

Let's focus on three aspects of rehearsal:

- why it's important
- how to rehearse
- the benefits of rehearsing

Why Is Rehearsing So Important?

When you do something for the first time, you will likely make a mistake or two. Wouldn't you rather make your mistakes in front of the mirror or a trusted colleague than in the room with a prospect or client?

Secondly, the mistakes we make often lead to better choices—or, at least, more interesting choices.

Practically, rehearsing allows you to understand the storyline from beginning to end. You can decide whether you are delivering the right message or if you've been derailed by a side story.

Effective Rehearsal Techniques

Run-through: As discussed, do a table read, as actors do when they have a new script.

1. **Adjust the semantics:** Make sure all the words are part of your everyday vocabulary.
2. **Tighten:** Cut out the extra words.
3. **Figure out the emotion underpinning the message:** Is this good news? Or a cautionary tale?
4. **Do the stage work:** Understand the room, the technology, the visibility of slides, and the acoustics.
5. **Choose your transitions between subjects or speakers:** It's better to think of these in advance than leave them to chance when you are presenting.

What Are the Benefits of Rehearsal?

The more you understand your message and the language you want to use, the more easily you can adopt a conversational tone. This tone will keep you more genuine and relatable than an unnatural "presentation voice."

The more reps you give yourself, the greater your confidence will be when it's time to speak. You'll know your conclusion, you'll know the potential side conversations, and you'll be at ease navigating whatever might come up.

Your confidence will give you the ability to pivot and nimbly address whatever your audience most wants to spend time on while still maintaining control of the narrative.

Finally, you will have better performance quality if you've taken some time to think about where to stand, how to move, what gestures will illuminate your message, and how to use your voice as the appropriate soundtrack to your story.

There are even benefits to a bad rehearsal! You quickly learn what the potential pitfalls might be (for example, perhaps you can't pronounce a certain word). It will help you make the appropriate changes to elevate the presentation when you deliver it for real.

Plus, it's healthy to fail constructively. We are all too obsessed with being perfect all the time. It's better to learn when you're likely to fumble in rehearsal and figure out ways to be more confident when you're actually presenting. Or to simply anticipate moving past a tiny misstep and finish strongly, no matter what happens.

Speaking of time, that's the only negative I can think of regarding rehearsal. It does take time. But the rewards outweigh the inconvenience. And you can start to incorporate rehearsal in small doses. You can take five minutes to rehearse your introduction, and maybe three more to do the conclusion. Those "bookends" will give you great comfort at the two most difficult points of every presentation or meeting.

Rehearsal should become a priority in your preparation and development of key messages. Small amounts of time allotted to honing the message will yield big rewards. The bottom line is this: Done well or done poorly, rehearsal will improve your ultimate performance.

Know the Story, Not Just the Lines

Once, I was given the role of Lucy in the play *Dracula*. I used to act in my spare time to stay in touch with my creative side. The production was being performed in a local community theater.

We did a handful of performances over the course of two or three weeks. Early in the run, there were three of us onstage at one point:

the man playing my father, the man playing Dr. Van Helsing, and me. I said my line and was expecting the man playing Father to answer with his line. His line was meant to be something about my retiring to my room and resting.

Instead, Father started to give me a very excited rendition of his lines from the act *after* the intermission (that we hadn't had yet). He had gotten confused and lost his place. If I had answered his lines with the ones he was now expecting, we would have missed half the exposition of the story and had quite the scramble on our hands.

Because we had rehearsed, I knew what had to happen next for the story to make sense. And in the few seconds I had been reacting to all of this, I said out loud, "Father, wouldn't it be better if I just went to my room and took a rest?"

I will never forget his wide-eyed response as he realized what had just happened. He enthusiastically replied, "Yes, yes," then gave me his perfect line, and we got back on track.

When you know—through rehearsal—where you are supposed to land, you can get through, despite unexpected detours.

In the Room Where It Happens

Showtime. The meeting begins, the presentation starts, or the conversation ensues. When you are communicating, whether formally or informally, you are also observing. It's the real-time observation, reaction, adjustment, and pivot that keep your message alive and engaging.

Even when you are on a stage in a larger forum, you are still interacting with and responding to your audience. And in a smaller group conversation, the art of questioning and listening will keep the balance right and the information flowing. It's always about rapport.

Planning for Success

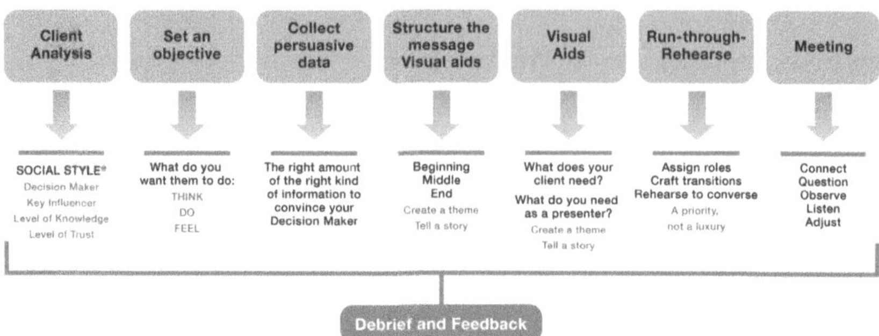

Source: CCB Communications, LLC.

The work is not done when the presentation ends. After the meeting, the off-site, or the conclusion of the conversation, you can use an outline like the example shown in figure 1 to debrief and give yourself or your colleagues feedback. When you do something brilliantly, you will see the foundation of that skill in the steps you took. If something went poorly, you'll see the missed step (and opportunity) when you review the process.

As you step into the world of impactful communication, recall the platter we discussed earlier—imagine yourself preparing for the most important dinner party of your life. Each step in this chapter is like selecting the finest ingredients, setting the table with care, and choosing the perfect wine to complement the meal. You've taken the time to understand your guests—what they like, how they'll feel most welcomed, and what will leave them wanting more. You've planned your menu with a clear purpose, gathered only the best ingredients, and rehearsed the timing to perfection. When the moment arrives, you present your creation with confidence, adjusting as you go to the feedback from your guests. And as the night ends, you reflect on what worked and what could be even better next time. Communication is no different—it's a craft, an art, and an opportunity to leave a lasting impression. Now, let's dive deeper into the tools that will make every "dinner party" you host an unforgettable success.

A word about using these planning steps. Using some is better than using none! I'm not asking you to immediately implement all of them. That would be, again, aiming for perfect pitch. You might start by spending a bit more time on understanding your audience and the context for the meeting, then rehearsing a wonderful conclusion that you can use as your anchor and landing spot to exit gracefully.

Whatever you work on first, stay with it for a while, until you feel some growth or some ease. We'll talk about this again when we focus on delivery skills. Little shifts are a big help.

3

KNOWING YOUR AUDIENCE

"If you don't know your audience, you'll never know how to communicate with them effectively."

—SIMON SINEK

I was first introduced to the SOCIAL STYLE® Model when I started as a communications consultant. This was when I first coined the term *simple magic* to describe the model's effectiveness. The power of this framework struck me instantly, and I often say, "I could draw this on a cocktail napkin for you and change your life in a few minutes." That's how impactful and transformative the concept can be.

But how did that knowledge unfold for me? When I joined Rogen International, I was sent to Sydney, Australia, to complete my "uni," i.e., the training program. During the program, my colleagues focused on communication techniques and how to run an effective training program. They introduced us to a model, based on the SOCIAL STYLE® material, and even in that oversimplified form, it was helpful. It was during this training that I began to see communication not as a one-size-fits-all skill but as something that needed to be tailored to the individual styles of those we work with.

The training at Rogen International was a revelation. It gave me a vocabulary and structure for improving communication—tools and language that I hadn't realized I was lacking. Before this training, I had simply assumed that people should adapt to me, without recognizing that I, too, needed to adapt my style to them. This new insight made me realize that effective communication isn't just about what you say—it's about how you say it and knowing when and why to adjust based on the listener's preferences.

To deepen my understanding, I sought out the source of the information and discovered the TRACOM Corporation, the original creator of the SOCIAL STYLE® Model. It cites a platinum rule, which is "Treat others the way they want to be treated."

There's a lot of power in that statement, especially when you apply it to those situations where communication isn't flowing smoothly. I'm sure you've experienced it: working with a colleague who seems impossible to connect with or having a conversation with a boss who doesn't quite hear you. Understanding the SOCIAL STYLE® Model could be the simple remedy to both of these common challenges. Observing and working with the unique communication styles of others and adjusting

Social Style Model™

The Social Style Model™ is a method that helps define a person's behavioral preferences. Understanding someone's behavioral patterns can give you a much better chance to connect, build rapport, and deliver messages that resonate with them. Source: Used with permission from the TRACOM Corporation.[3]

3 SOCIAL STYLE, The Social Intelligence Company, The Creator of SOCIAL STYLE, SOCIAL STYLE Model, and TRACOM are registered trademarks of the TRACOM Corporation.

your approach accordingly can create profound shifts in how you interact and collaborate.

Over the years, when I looked back on past work situations where I struggled to connect with certain individuals, it was easy to blame the other person. They made things difficult for me. But that was the wrong way to think about it. I just hadn't cracked the code of how to understand them and change my message so they could hear it.

Remember the example I gave you in chapter 2, when the boss gave me my review and said, "You're too nice"?

His assessment left me dumbfounded. What about the many successes? The great hires? The hurdles jumped over? The brilliant ideas? The great management? I felt completely invisible to this man. I asked myself, *Why is being nice a bad thing?* It's a strong value that I hold in life, but it doesn't take away from my brilliance as a leader. How could he miss all of that?

In hindsight, I reacted too "nicely." I packed up mentally and left the bank less than a year later.

Had I known how to work with the Social Style Model™, I would have been able to fix the confusion. I could have told him what he had missed in a way that would have resonated with him and possibly have changed his opinion of me. I might have remained a banker!

What was at play here was a simple matter of needing to understand one's audience and set clear communication objectives. The Social Style Model™ helps you identify your audience's needs and expectations.

This is why I recommend that, at the start of a meeting (not a formal presentation), you are always prepared with a short introduction of yourself, then immediately go into inquiry: "What's top of your mind today? Do you have a burning question? What are you looking for in a business partner?" Any questions that will get your prospect talking so that you can learn about who they are and where they are (emotionally) in that meeting.

We need to create space—and silence—so our audience can tell us about themselves. You could allot the first minutes of every meeting to paying attention to how they are delivering their messages as well as what they are saying. You listen to the very words they use because a person's semantics can reveal a great deal about their priorities and the way they think.

Observable Behaviors Versus Personality

It's important to stress that the Social Style Model™ is not a personality test but a behavioral model. One looks at the observable behaviors, what someone does or says, how that might change when they are with others, and what the predictable patterns of behavior might be (Cathy always uses her hands when she talks, etc.). These behaviors are like the crust of a pie—it's what you see on the outside.

Understanding how to flex to these different behaviors gives you the ability to cut to the center of the pie and get to the juicy, delicious filling—the equivalent of someone's ideas, values, hopes, and dreams. According to TRACOM's research, this versatility makes communicators 88 percent more effective at working with others, 74 percent more likely to improve conflict situations, and 71 percent better at working with difficult relationships. As versatility improves, so does performance. Let's take a look at these four SOCIAL STYLE® designations.

Each one of us has ALL of them: amiable, analytical, driving, and expressive. We just possess them in varying degrees. We each have one that is the dominant way we express ourselves, but the idea is to be versatile in using all four. The art of using the model involves observing where a person is in that moment and flexing your communication so they can understand you better.

Versatility is the key to successfully using the model. You show your versatility through your image, your presentation skills, your competence, and your ability to take and receive feedback.

Versatility is at the heart of how we create rapport. Having rapport helps create and sustain long-lasting business relationships.

You're doing this instinctively already, I'll warrant. If we were in a conference room together and it was getting close to the end of an hour, you might hear me start to get more clipped in my responses—"Yes," "That's right," "Mm-hmm"—as I anticipate finishing the meeting on time. You might then say, "We're done here; why don't we end early?" sensing the need to wrap things up. Rapport is a kind of harmony of style.

Traits and Judgments

Start by noticing what others say and do. Are they quiet or loud? Do they lean in or lean back? Do they make a lot of eye contact or avoid looking into your eyes?

What people say and do should be neutral, but as part of our natural inclinations, we assign traits and make judgments about people based on *how* they are communicating.

Assertiveness

This work can begin with observing a person's level of assertiveness. Are they an asker or a teller? There are those who ask, those who exhibit a combination of asking with some telling, those who prefer telling with some asking, and those who tell. Does the person start every sentence with a question? Or do they bark orders in a declarative fashion?

During my time at Rogen, I was once summoned to my CEO's office. I went in gladly, since I had just secured a great account. I was pretty confident she was going to tell me how wonderful I was.

She started the meeting by saying, "You're making me crazy."

Startled, I asked, "What do you mean?"

She said, "Every time you walk into my office, you say, 'Do you have a minute?'"

I was shocked. *What could be wrong with that?* I thought to myself. *I was raised right. I was just being polite, taking into consideration all the other stresses she had, the projects on her desk, and the possibility that she had other priorities.*

She continued, "When you start like that, I immediately disengage. It makes you seem weak."

I was losing the first few seconds of every meeting with her! I was asking, and she needed me to be telling her what I wanted. Properly advised, I set out to address her with more of a Tell Assertive style. I would stop outside her office and say to myself, as a way to prepare, "Don't ask! Don't ask!"

That resulted in my entering her room and saying, "I NEED YOU NOW" or "SIGN THIS."

I wasn't very natural at it, and it felt as if I were screaming at her. She didn't flinch. What resonated as yelling to me simply resonated as confidence to her.

It was uncomfortable for me to speak in that way during those early trials. It was very far from how I'd been communicating all my life. Yet, it was so effective with her. She even started to talk about my strengths to others on the team. I hadn't changed who I was—*just how I was engaging in conversations about it.*

In fact, it so resonated with her that she only realized after seven or eight Tell entrances what I was doing. Approvingly, she said, "You've changed."

I said, "I'm a good student!"

I am still grateful to her because she helped me access my Tell voice. It's the voice I use when I want to be assertive, take the lead, or simply save time.

It's important to note that all the while I was learning how to do this better, she would approach me with, "Cathy, do you have a moment?" She was more skilled and knew that, at the beginning of my learning, a Tell command might seem aggressive to me.

It's Not Just the Words

Assertiveness manifests in not just verbal behaviors but also in nonverbal behaviors. You'll want to focus on what people say or do. When speaking, look at these three areas:

- **Pace of speech:** Are they slower or faster than others in the room?
- **Quantity of speech:** Are they giving you fewer or more words?
- **Volume of speech:** Are they quieter or louder?

What about their nonverbal behaviors?

- **Use of hands:** Are they relaxed or directive?
- **Body posture:** Are they leaning back or leaning forward?
- **Eye contact:** Is their eye contact less direct or more direct?

Overall, people who are manifesting Ask Assertive behaviors will demonstrate less energy, move more slowly, gesture less vigorously, speak more softly, use less eye contact, and decide with more deliberation. They are generally less comfortable with conflict and confrontation and will demonstrate anger less quickly.

People who are manifesting Tell Assertive behaviors will exude more energy, gesture more vigorously, use more intense eye contact, speak more rapidly, make quick decisions, and be more direct. They are generally more comfortable with conflict and confrontation and can demonstrate anger more quickly.

An important reminder: There is no one right way to be. It's just effective—and polite—to meet someone closer to where they are in that moment.

I am asked to help people speak up in meetings and at the workplace all the time. It's easy to start with helping the client acquire a more Driving or Expressive style, but we should remember to also examine the culture, team, and circumstances that surround that individual—have we created enough safety, or simply space, for team members to step forward?

Another common complaint I hear from senior team members, particularly investment committee members, is that presenters will offer a thorough talk about a prospective investment but never once assert that they themselves would really like to do the deal. By passively presenting facts and figuratively stepping back to let the seniors make the decision, they have made themselves unremarkable and, perhaps, unnecessary. The more senior members of the team want to learn how the newer members think; they might find favor in them for their boldness, even if they say no to the deal. Risk nothing; win nothing.

Risk nothing; win nothing.

Responsiveness

The next element to observe is someone's responsiveness. What you're looking for here is the degree to which you can read someone's emotions on their face or in their aspect.

There are some who are more controlling of their emotions, some who are controlling with some emoting, some who are emoting with some controlling, and some who are more emoting. Again, you'll want to observe what they say and do:

- **Emotion in voice:** Are they using less inflection or more inflection?
- **Subjects of speech:** Do they talk about tasks or people?
- **Form of descriptives:** Do they use more facts and data or more stories and opinions?

Emote Responsive people may express their feelings more openly, have a more friendly affect, use more vocal inflection, tell more anecdotes and stories, talk about human aspects of issues, apply less structure in their use of time, and prefer working with others.

Control Responsive people tend to be less open about their feelings, appear more reserved, show less interest in small talk, use more facts and logic than anecdotes, impose more structure in their use of time, and often prefer to work alone.

Assertiveness Behaviors

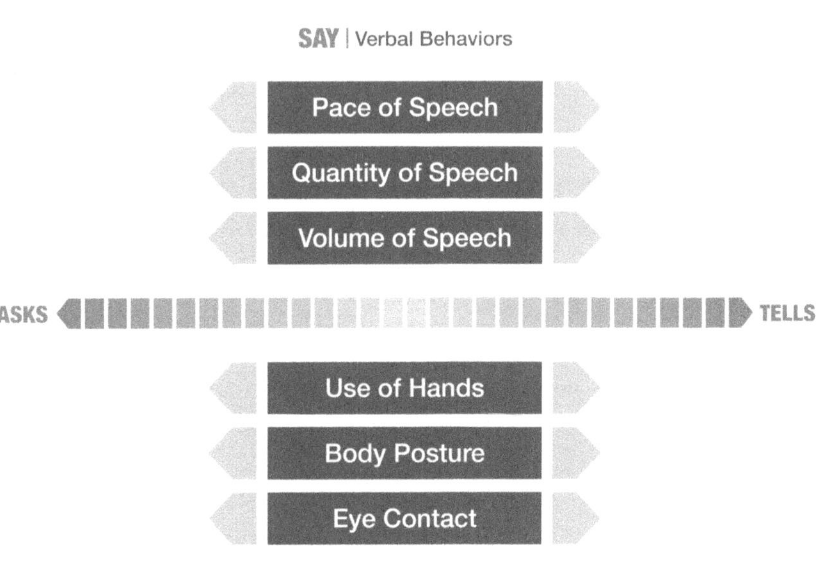

This chart illustrates the verbal (say) and nonverbal (do) behaviors as they manifest on the Assertiveness spectrum. Used with permission from the TRACOM Corporation.

Think of the term *poker face* and the person who doesn't show emotion or reaction compared to the person whose face changes with nearly every thought.

As an Emoting communicator, I used to get my feelings hurt if a more Controlling communicator wouldn't smile back at me or respond warmly in a meeting. "Why don't they like me?" That was my need, not theirs. Now that I am able to recognize it as a style preference, not a declaration of dislike, it doesn't faze me at all when someone's face is serious. I instead recognize that they might find my expressions to be over the top, so I calm my facial animation and meet them with more stillness.

It's important to remove the words *good* and *bad* when describing styles; there's just *similar* or *different*.

Having the versatility to flex your style to be more similar to that of your listener is a courtesy and a skill.

Responsiveness Behaviors

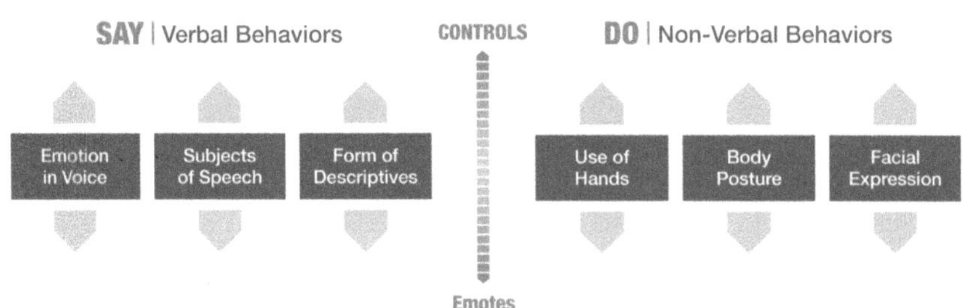

This chart illustrates the verbal (say) and nonverbal (do) behaviors as they manifest on the Responsiveness spectrum. Used with permission from the TRACOM Corporation.

Let's look at each SOCIAL STYLE® designation's attributes, how they will behave, and what you can do to be more versatile and flex effectively (see figure 3). The goal is to build better connections, understanding, and rapport.

SOCIAL STYLE Model™

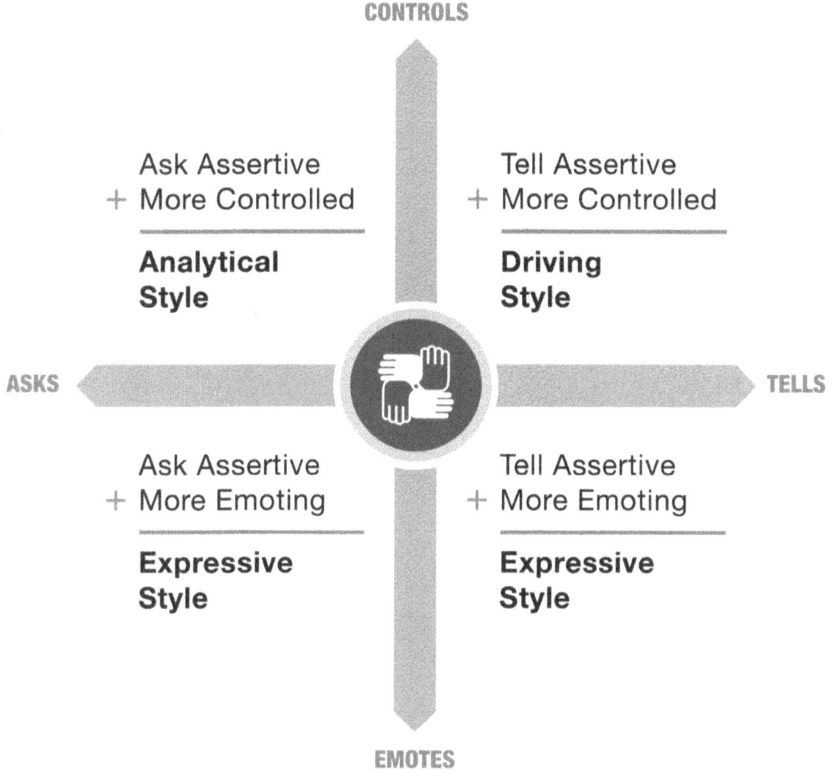

The SOCIAL STYLE® designations.

Now that we know the name of each of the SOCIAL STYLE® quadrants (figure 4), in the next chapter, we'll focus on how to recognize when someone is displaying that style and how best to flex to their preference.

4

FLEXING TO THE SOCIAL STYLE® MODEL

"Speak comfortable words."

—WILLIAM SHAKESPEARE

In a world driven by communication and connection, the ability to adapt isn't just a nice skill to have; it's a leadership essential. Whether we're collaborating with colleagues, leading a team, or navigating a difficult conversation, our success often depends on how well we can tune into others' needs, preferences, and behavioral cues.

That's where Versatility comes in. It's the art of flexing, of adjusting your communication and approach to better align with someone else's SOCIAL STYLE®. Think of it as emotional intelligence in action. It's not about changing who you are; it's about being mindful and intentional in how you show up for others.

The SOCIAL STYLE Model™ provides a powerful lens through which to understand these differences. By learning to recognize and respond to the behavioral patterns of others, whether they're more Assertive or Responsive, we can reduce tension, build trust faster, and increase our influence.

Before we explore how to flex with each style, let's take a moment to understand how these styles tend to manifest in everyday interactions.

Here are some descriptions of how each style manifests.

Driving Style

I always say that this is the style that would be saying, "Follow me into battle!" or "Let's get it done now!" People with this style need results, and they are oriented to action. But they might need to work on listening more.

What Will You Observe?

Driving communicators will

- be faster paced;
- make efforts to set the pace;
- be less concerned with the value of relationships;
- work in the present time frame;
- tend to direct the actions of others, whether or not they are the leader; and
- tend to avoid inaction.

Clues that might indicate someone has a dominant Driving style are the following:

They may take control of the meeting; ask for the bottom line; use short, powerful sentences; and steer the course of the conversation. They might even snap their fingers or tap their foot out of impatience at any pace that is slower than theirs. They will disagree and even readily engage in conflict to defend their position.

How to Flex to the Driving Style

In order to flex to the Driving style, I recommend that my clients shorten their statements, increase the power in their voice (get louder), use bullet points, and be energetic. They should focus on results and be clear and brief. They should state their opinions and take a stand to defend them, if necessary. They should be efficient with time, and, optimally, end the meeting early.

Early in my time at Rogen International, I was asked to run a two-day Selling Skills class for a large investment bank. I was to teach the class to eight senior bankers who would ultimately decide if the program had merit enough to be repeated throughout the bank.

I started the class by saying, "Hello, my name is Cathy Bonczek, and I'm here to run your Selling Skills program."

A woman at the opposite end of the conference room table shouted out, "I've been doing sales for twenty years! What could you possibly teach me about sales?"

You could see the figurative gauntlet hurtling through the air at me.

I had to immediately augment my Driving style. I replied, "Here's what I'm going to do. I will own you for the next three hours. If you don't like what I teach you, I will leave you at lunchtime. I will give you a refund and you'll gain a day and a half back on your calendar."

I delivered this reply, in my strong chest voice, while using very intense eye contact with each person in the room.

Their reply was, "That's great—we'll be out of here by lunch!"

I then delivered all the information I had in a Driving style: "I need a volunteer. *You*, come here."

Tip: When I want to access my Driving style, I clip my sentences. I drop into my deeper chest voice, I increase the intensity of my eye contact, and I get ready to disagree and defend my opinions. It's such a refreshingly strong way to deliver messages! It's a power play.

At noon, I turned to the room and said, "All good? Am I coming back after lunch?"

And they said, "This is great. Yes, we're coming back after lunch."

They left the room, and I took a very deep breath. I was exhausted because it had taken more effort for me to deliver in the Driving style, but I was very pleased to have given them what they wanted.

At the end of the day, I asked again, "Am I coming back tomorrow?" They said, "Yes."

By the end of the two days, they suggested that I would be a great hire for their team. I thanked them but couldn't say no fast enough. I knew that I couldn't sustain that much effort every day.

This was one of my first experiences of the power in flexing to your audience's style.

Expressive Style

The Expressive style is close to my heart because this is my dominant style. Remember, we all have all four styles, just to different degrees. People whose Expressive style is dominant need personal approval, and they take action spontaneously. Their development need is to check their energy and pace.

What Will You Observe?

Expressive communicators will

- talk quickly and gesture actively,
- be confident and conversational,
- be dramatic in style and words,
- interrupt and/or make faces, and
- talk about gut reactions.

You might recognize an Expressive person communicating with flair and saying something like, "I have an idea, and it's going to be great!" I always say my strong dominance in this style explains why I like to be on stage, standing in the spotlight. You'll often hear me say, "Let me tell you a story ..." or talk about how much I *love* a book or play.

You will notice their faster pace, willingness to get involved, eagerness to work with others, and future-focused observations. You might also sense some impulsivity.

How to Flex to the Expressive Style

Pick up your pace, make direct eye contact, and be prepared to make a spontaneous decision. Allow time for brainstorming and use the language of emotion.

Amiable Style

I like to think of the Amiable style as the kinder, gentler style. The Amiable communicator needs personal security and is oriented to relationships. They naturally build and support great teams. Often, they need to work at initiating, taking the step to the front of the room, and stating their opinion.

You might hear them say something like, "One for all and all for one!"

What Will You Observe?

The Amiable communicator is likely to be slower paced and make a lot of effort to relate to others. They will be less dramatic in how they speak, and it may seem as if they are less concerned about effecting change. They seek harmony and consensus, and they have to work at taking the lead in meetings. They will avoid conflict.

You'll see them gather opinions and encourage others to speak. They will tell personal stories readily and place great emphasis on rapport.

How to Flex to the Amiable Style

Start by establishing rapport and setting a moderate pace. Use your dulcet tones and invite conversation. Listen attentively and without judgment. Make mutual decisions. When communicating in the Amiable style, make many references to the team, the viewpoints of the many, and how it will feel to work together. Show eagerness to include all voices in a dialogue; these communicators are very aware of the human aspects of every meeting.

You will recognize from my earlier story about asking my boss, "Do you have a minute?" that I was manifesting my Amiable style, even though Expressive is more dominant in my profile. This makes sense because the two styles are adjacent and have a common focus on people and relationships. I believe my habit of communicating in an Amiable style stemmed from a desire to be nonconfrontational and diplomatic, but it didn't always serve me well.

My boss, quick to say "No," was replying in her preferred Driving style. Amiable and Driving—diagonally across from each other with no adjacencies—have a greater distance to go to connect.

I have many conversations with executives on how to balance the Amiable and Driving styles. Often, forceful leaders feel the need to soften their communication to prevent being seen as aggressive or harsh. I think this is an important skill for everyone to have, and much depends on the expectations of the firm (does it have a kind culture or an action-first culture?) and the context of the communication (is it a meet and greet or an emergency decision session?).

Analytical Style

The Analytical style is a measured, more controlled style. Like the Amiable style, the Analytical is more of an asking style. People whose dominant style is Analytical are oriented to thinking, and they have a need to be accurate. They often need to work on declaring their decisions or opinions (and not just continuing to gather data).

They will be inclined to say something like, "Just the facts, please!"

What Will You Observe?

Analytical communicators will be slower paced and very organized. They will use or follow an agenda readily, and they will take time to come to an agreement. They will focus more on the process, the research, and the historical viewpoint than on interpersonal relationships.

How to Flex to the Analytical Style

When speaking with an Analytical communicator, be moderately paced and organized, logical, and exact in your details. Offer a measured balance of pros and cons and allow time for them to think and assess. Be comfortable with long pauses or silences.

Look at the diagonal quadrant from your dominant style.

With all my energy and spontaneous communicating (you thought I was going to say combustion, didn't you?), you can see why the style that is diagonally opposite mine on the chart, the Analytical style, would pose the most difficulty for me. It's hard for me to slow down, be more methodical, reduce the energy, and diminish the dramatic statements. I remind myself to start with an agenda and stick to it. I am very conscious of outlining expected time frames and sharing facts and statistics about whatever topic I am addressing. I also quiet my inner *bounce* and slow my pace. This helps me think in a more methodical way and deliver information in a way that is logical and precise.

In turn, an Analytical communicator might find me a little too perky or emotional and too ready to veer away from the set agenda. They might find it challenging to speed up or follow a tangent.

I am reminded of a boss—let's call him Bob—who once told me that my meetings weren't effective. I was startled, since I was getting a lot of buzz in the firm about how I ran meetings and how jazzed my team was to meet its goals and challenges. We were fast becoming the team to watch. What could he think was missing?

It turns out I was missing an agenda—*for him*. I worked instinctively off the roundtable offerings I received when I started every meeting with, "What's on your mind?" I would get a sense in that brief discussion of the top priority of the team, and we'd start there, then continue to the next topic.

He felt it showed a lack of preparedness on my part, but I argued that I was prepared to talk about anything that would come up. All that being said, I simply shifted to creating an agenda and dropping it off on his deck before every meeting. I shared it at the beginning of each team meeting for any other communicator who needed to know there was logic underpinning my free-flowing exposition.

Similarly, the Amiable and Driving styles have fewer points of commonality, and people for whom these styles are dominant may find it more challenging to connect.

Think back to my example of my boss telling me that I was "too nice." He was using a Driving style, and I was using an Amiable style. If I'd known then what to do, I might have said, "You're crazy! You've missed the most important parts of what I've done. Yes, I'm nice, but it's an asset, not a liability. You've got it all wrong."

He may have respected my moxie, and, as I said, I might still be a banker!

Please don't expect people to communicate in one way only. We all have a style that is more dominant, but we all have them *all.*

You might be thinking, *I won't know who I'm meeting with until I walk into the room.* As you ask your opening questions, assess how people answer them. What words have they used? How much energy are they exhibiting? Where's their eye contact?

Your goal is to figure out where people are right now and respond in kind.

Make your best assessment and change your message accordingly. Be prepared to shift to a different style as the meeting progresses and trust grows.

I often say that communication is as much about observation as it is about delivering a message. Listening carefully to the people you engage with will give you strong indications of how they like to give and get their information.

Let's take it one step further. As you begin, it's important to simply start noticing how people are communicating. I often say, "Watch me toward the end of a session. You'll see me use more of a Driving style because I am determined to end on time." You may already be noticing this in others and instinctively shifting to "Let's wrap it up, or it's time to bring it to a close" when you sense this across the table.

Remember, there is no "best style"; they are all equally effective. It bears repeating: We all have all the styles within us. The goal is to find ways to express ourselves in all four.

More Advanced Work with the Styles

After some time, when you've been observing the SOCIAL STYLE® of others for a while, try to flex more quickly. In your meetings, listen to how your clients or colleagues ask questions. Try to answer the questions in kind, in the same styles in which they were asked.

In other words, if the question is asked in the Analytical Style, respond with facts and precision. If the question is asked in the Driving style, give a terse, bottom-line response.

Adapting the SOCIAL STYLE Model™ Through Technology

Voicemail

Imagine you have telephoned a friend and you get their outgoing message. Here's how each style might craft that voicemail message.

Expressive

Beep.
"Hi, I'm off having an exciting adventure! When I call you back, I'll tell you the whole story!"

Amiable

Beep.
"Hello, I am so sorry that I missed your call. I will call you back as soon as I am able so that we can catch up properly. Thank you for calling!"

Analytical

Beep.
"Hello, today is Monday the fifth. I will be out of the office until three forty-five this afternoon. Please leave a message of no more than two minutes, and I will call you back at four o'clock. Thank you."

Driving

Beep.
"You know what to do."

The key is to leave a message in a similar style to the outgoing message.

Zoom

How do you assess someone's SOCIAL STYLE® when you are on Zoom?

You will have to adapt to the loss of some of your nonverbal cues (although, I can often tell when a person is tapping their foot from impatience, even if they're on Zoom—their shoulders will give it away).

When on Zoom or Teams, the first part of the conversation and the greetings become even more important: You should listen carefully to the speed, volume, and number of words each person uses. Listen for specific words that might hint at their overall values. If someone values accuracy, you might try using your Analytical style to provide them with details and lots of proof.

You use all the tools you can. At the onset of the online meeting, I do stage-setting and housekeeping:

I start by telling everyone present that I will forward a copy of the PowerPoint deck. That usually relieves most Analytically inclined communicators.

I often present with a fellow coach who takes on the "watch the chat" role. She will read and respond to chat comments, which is something that's often hard for me to do when I'm presenting or modeling a technique. We make sure the participants know who she is and that she can be their response coordinator.

When the number of participants is manageable, it's a good idea to do a round-the-table introduction. This allows everyone in attendance to have a voice.

Then you listen carefully and observe: Who responds to every comment or question the facilitator makes? Who challenges? Who nods continuously but doesn't ever unmute? You call on participants and watch how they physically respond while you listen to the words they use. It is productive to lengthen the pauses between sentences in your presentation—to give everyone time to interject if they would like to.

I mentioned at the beginning of the chapter that I truly love working with the SOCIAL STYLE Model™. It has greatly impacted my ability to deliver messages and receive messages without emotional disruption. If someone barks at me, I don't immediately feel reproved or attacked; I simply note it and increase my own assertiveness. Constantly observing my audience helps keep me tactical, not vulnerable.

At your next meeting, listen to your clients and/or colleagues. Capture the words they use and the actions they display, and see if you can determine which style they are using most frequently.

To practice further, assume you are trying to hire a talented individual to join your team. Invite them in four different ways: Driving, Expressive, Amiable, and Analytical. This will help you flex to your version of each style.

Here are the main tips and takeaways:

1. There is no best style.
2. Style is not personality.
3. Your style is a theme in your behavior.
4. Your style has growth actions.

Source: Tracom

Cross-Cultural Communication

As we work more and more globally, it's important to take different cultural styles into account. American communicators are often considered bold and direct. TRACOM writes that the Chinese culture is often considered to be even bolder and even more direct.

The SOCIAL STYLE Model™ is universal, but take extra consideration with understanding the influence of cultural mores, etiquette, and expectations for each quadrant.

As we wrap up this chapter, it's important to remember that the foundation of effective communication lies in flexibility and adaptability. Communication is not a one-size-fits-all approach. It's about understanding that each individual you interact with brings their own perspective, needs, and communication style to the table. By adapting your approach to meet them where they are, whether through adjusting your tone, pace, or the way you present information, you can build stronger connections and navigate even the most challenging conversations with confidence.

To deepen your engagement with this material, I encourage you to practice the strategies we've discussed. Role-playing scenarios, for example, can be an excellent way to put these concepts into action. By stepping into different communication styles and adjusting your responses accordingly, you'll gain invaluable experience that will enhance your ability to flex to any audience.

Ultimately, the goal is to build not only the theoretical knowledge of communication styles but also the practical skills that allow you to adapt to any situation with ease. The more you practice this flexibility, the more natural it will become to switch between styles and communicate effectively, no matter whom you're speaking with or the context in which you're engaging.

With these tools in hand, you'll be equipped to master the art of communication and connect with any audience—whether it's colleagues, clients, or team members—ensuring that your message resonates and your influence grows. Keep in mind that effective communication is a continual learning process, and the more you practice, the more adept you'll become at navigating conversations with anyone, anywhere.

I take inspiration from the story of Mark Twain. He is so familiar to us as a literary and cultural figure, yet we don't often take into consideration that he worked very hard to become that renowned orator and beloved figure. He was drawn to that type of work due to misfortune and the need to make a living in his later years.

On a visit to the Mark Twain house, built in 1870 and now a museum, I was amazed at the abundance of articles, books, and opinions Mark Twain had written in his lifetime. Like many others, I know of him for just a few of his works: *The Adventures of Tom Sawyer*, *The Adventures of Huckleberry Finn*, and *A Connecticut Yankee in King Arthur's Court.*

His real name was Samuel Clemens, and he claimed that his nom de plume was taken from an old Mississippi riverboat captain who wasn't using it anymore. "Mark twain!" is actually the call made to assure a captain that his steamboat was floating in water that was two fathoms deep.

An alternative theory is that the name was derived from Clemens's habit of walking into a bar and shouting, "Mark Twain!" meaning, "Give me two whiskeys, and make two chalk marks on the board." I like the riverboat myth better.

His life story is fascinating. I learned about his ability to work hard and to write about everything he experienced. I read more of his satirical wit and grew to appreciate his courage and intelligence. I also learned that he was a dedicated husband and father and spent time spinning tales with his children whenever he could.

As a writer and an orator, he was funny, but not always kind. When he saw actions that he thought were deplorable, he spoke up, frequently and loudly, to condemn those actions (such as imperialism). He even changed his mind publicly, which is something we don't see often enough today.

I learned that he had invested heavily ($300,000 in 1887) in an invention that was a mechanical typesetter meant to speed up the printing process. It was called the Paige Compositor, and fewer than six machines were ever made. It was unsuccessful and too complicated to work consistently. In fact, Cornell University relinquished one of the few machines in existence to be made into scrap metal during World War II. Twain lost most of his money on this investment. He was known for his wisdom, but that didn't translate into venture success.[4]

After declaring bankruptcy, Twain started traveling the world again, giving lectures to recuperate some of his lost income. Over the course of several years, he made all the money back and cleared every debt. I marvel at his resilience and integrity, even when faced with a financial defeat. After declaring bankruptcy, he did not have a legal obligation to return payments to his debtors, yet he did.

He was also once considered the most popular man in the United States, loved his family very much, and lost all but one of his children in his lifetime. Having written his autobiography, he asked that it be published one hundred years after his death.

Even as I write these words, I saw him quoted on social media twice today: He is ubiquitous, yet we've gotten comfortable in our perception of him. He's the man in the white suit with wild, white hair. I am intrigued to go deeper, read more of his work, and walk alongside him in a different way.

Why? Because Mark Twain demonstrates the idea that what we say and how we say it can leave lasting impressions. You don't have to know a person well to be moved by them or inspired by them. They just have to be authentic for you to connect with them in a deep way.

This is why it's important not to be glib but rather to speak your opinion, loudly and bravely. Originality can lead you to be intriguing, to be listened to, and to be remembered.

What would your legacy be if you could choose it?

---

4 "Mark Twain Loses Money Backing the Paige Compositor," Jeremy Norman's HistoryofInformation.com, June 11, 2025, www.historyofinformation.com/detail.php?id=4709.

5

SETTING YOUR OBJECTIVE

"Success is the sum of small efforts, repeated day in and day out."

—ROBERT COLLIER

The second step to preparing your message is figuring out in advance what you want your audience to think, do, or feel as a result of your communication. Most of my clients have skipped this important clarifying step because they have just assumed it was all so obvious.

It's not obvious; it's just left to interpretation unless you craft it. Without intention and practice, your automatic responses will take over and you'll just be winging it. You have more power than you think to manifest and make a lasting impression.

Remember, we just talked about the importance of liking the people we work with. It's OK if you want your prospect or client to think well of you. After all, you've spent years acquiring the skill and talent to do an amazing job. Why not let them know that's part of what you bring to the table?

You need to ask yourself, "What do I want my client to think, do, or feel at the end of this conversation?"

Do you want them to hold a new or different belief?

Do you want them to be intrigued?

Do you want them to trust you?

One of my clients was preparing for a meeting, and I asked, "What do you want your prospect to *think* about the proposal when you're done presenting?" She said, "I never really thought about it, but I want them to think that we've designed a portfolio that's better than any other they've seen."

"What else?" I asked. She thought about it for a while, then said, "And I want them to think that we can repeat that with our next fund and the one after that."

Which led me to ask, "What do you want them to do, as a result?"

She said, "I want them to write me a big check on the spot!" And she laughed.

Knowing that it doesn't often happen that immediately, I asked, "Realistically, what do you want them to *do* after you're done presenting?"

She said, "I want them to ask a few questions and schedule another meeting for us to go into more detail. I want them to tell me honestly how much they are thinking about investing and who else is in the running for their money."

I asked, "How do you want them to *feel* about you, the meeting, and your firm?"

She said, "We usually just assume that they will like us!"

I said, "You need to plan for that."

As we talked, she expressed her desire for the clients to feel confident in their decision to work with them—trusting their expertise and seeing the unique value they offered. She wanted them to leave the meeting excited, not only about the service but also about the potential financial benefits of their portfolio.

Her honesty about her expectations for the meeting caught my attention. She was surprised at how high those expectations were, and I reminded her that, by clearly planning for those outcomes, she'd increase the likelihood of achieving them.

That's when I turned the conversation inward, urging her to consider both the business objectives and her personal ones.

Our discussion yielded a moment of realization. While it's essential to focus on the goals and deliverables, it's equally important to think about your personal brand and how your presence can shape the experience for others. We hadn't just discussed the business outcomes—we had touched on how she could leave a lasting impact through her own approach and influence during the meeting.

I shared with her my belief that we should all hold our brand, or our definition of what we represent in our working world, close to our hearts in every meeting, conversation, or presentation.

The fastest way to augment your personal brand is to describe yourself using just five words. If someone asked you, "Who are you?" and you could only offer them five words, what would those five words be?

It's not five words for life, but you should have five words for every meeting, presentation, or pitch.

I encourage my clients to be aspirational and bold in how they define themselves. The point is that they should talk to themselves in a positive way to help ensure the further development of these traits.

It is the same for all the other words we might use to describe ourselves. When you know something to be true about yourself, it will be a part of your spoken word and overall impact.

My five words change a little bit depending on the audience and how well they know me already, but one word that never leaves my list is *love.* I love what I do and the clients I get to work with, and I believe that love is a powerful force for good in the world. I want people to know that about me when they work with me. I want them to feel that I have their backs and am there to help them.

My most frequent words to describe myself are *intelligent, creative, charismatic*, and *authentic*. At other times, I use *communication master* and *innovator*. It's important to pick words that have meaning to you.

Remember my role in *Dracula*? When I went to try out, I knew I wanted to play the lead role of Lucy. I rehearsed for the audition with my acting teacher, Janet Sarno. She was the one who taught me the power of holding an intention that wasn't spoken but underpinned in all my words and actions. She suggested I use the word *sexy* as a mantra. I was thinking *sexy, sexy, sexy* in a running sequence while saying my lines. This was the part of the play when Lucy was very prim and proper and not supposed to be overtly sexy.

At the end of my audition, the director yelled, "That was so sexy!"

And I got the part.

Imagine walking into your next meeting and saying to yourself, *confident, confident, confident*, and having that be the backdrop to everything you say in the meeting. The likelihood is high that others in the room will perceive you as confident.

There's a power in owning how you want the world to see you, and saying your words to yourself is a good way to manifest those characteristics in your meeting. No, you don't describe yourself by listing your words! You show them in the way that you engage with your audience throughout the meeting.

I do recommend sharing your five words as a good way to begin a performance discussion with your manager, however. Imagine asking your boss to describe you in five words and then sharing your choices with them; that will make for a very interesting conversation!

You won't need to tell someone that you're humble; they will learn it by what you say and don't say.

You won't need to tell an audience that you are passionate about your work; they will see it and feel it as you talk about the deal.

Taking the time to walk through what you want the outcome of each interaction to be is a way of increasing your confidence, augmenting your brand, and achieving what you really want to happen.

The messenger matters. Business is still founded on relationships, trust, and chemistry. That's what makes being a wonderfully imperfect human communicator so magical.

6

PERSUASION

"Simplicity is the ultimate sophistication."

—LEONARDO DA VINCI

Let's get this straight—more is not more. In fact, more is confusing, overwhelming, and downright counterproductive. If you've ever been in a meeting where the presenter opens a PowerPoint presentation and the screen fills with a blizzard of words, numbers, and charts, you know exactly what I mean. It's as though the presenter believes that the more they show, the more convincing they'll be. Spoiler alert: They're wrong.

In my many years of working with clients, particularly in the financial sector, I've seen it all. Pitch decks, fundraising proposals, and informational presentations—each one stuffed with enough text to make your eyes glaze over. My personal favorite? The classic four pie charts on one page. If you're guilty of this, I have a friendly piece of advice: Stop.

I call it "bringing the encyclopedia." It's when you try to shove everything, and I mean *everything*, into one slide or deck. Let me be clear: No one wants to sit through a page-by-page, detailed rendition of your pitch book.

Here's the thing—when I suggest you streamline your message and make it more concise, you'll probably push back. You'll say, "But we have to send this deck ahead of time! We need to be prepared to leave behind the full details after the meeting!"

I get it. But here's the challenge: How do you focus on the key points that elevate your message instead of burying it? By keeping it simple, focusing on clarity, and eliminating the clutter, you'll discover that less truly is more—more engaging, more persuasive, and more memorable.

It's time to rethink what you're presenting and how you're presenting it. Let's dive in. I went on a sales call with a client many years ago when I was at Rogen. The client needed my help. They'd mandated that no deck could be longer than twenty-five pages. What happened? They pulled out four decks. Each one was twenty-five pages long.

This client brought us in to teach their sales leaders how to be more concise and use only one deck. Neither the "send before" nor the "leave behind" is appropriate for the meeting or presentation. We should use different tools—the ones that are specifically helpful to your audience and their communication preferences, and to you as the speaker. You need to understand what your prospect or client really wants, not just what they say they want. What do you need to keep the conversation going forward but natural at the same time?

I was brought in once to do pitch consulting for an investment banking team that was trying to win a significant piece of business. The team was based in the United States, and the work would be done in Europe in a fairly remote location. Before the pitch, I asked, "How important is it for you to emphasize how you will have 'feet on the ground' in their location?" The team dismissed my concern, saying, "We've already told them we have people nearby and will be able to handle their business."

When they lost the pitch, the reason cited was that there had been no emphasis on how they would provide support locally. My team was crushed because they felt they had superior resources and that their prospect had made a poor choice. They had attempted to persuade the prospect with facts alone, missing the emotional underpinning of the questions about support.

Less Is More

The German architect Ludwig Mies van der Rohe is credited with the principle of less is more. In modern design, this principle involves removing superfluous elements to enhance the clarity of the concept.

In philosophy, it means that simplicity can lead to a more fulfilling and meaningful life.

In minimalism (the lifestyle), it represents the choice to make do with fewer things and serve people and the planet with more attention and time.

In minimalism (the abstract art form), it means a departure from the conventional aesthetic and the use of geometric or simple forms.

In fashion, it means you emphasize simplicity and clarity. It also means focusing on quality and prioritizing elegance, functionality, and a sense of harmony.

In makeup, it means that a natural look is more attractive than an overly made-up look.

In acting, it means emphasizing the economy of effort used to produce a performance.

In literature, it means something like *The Sun Also Rises* by Ernest Hemingway: clean and spare language to set the stage and the story.

In business discourse, it means cutting to the bottom-line message and making it so clear that it's indisputable what the speaker meant. It translates to clarity, confidence, and charisma.

In all of the above examples, the common thread is that, to get to "less is more," you must decide it's a concept worth embracing. Then you have to practice it, make a concerted effort, and refine, refine, refine.

I urge you to embrace the concept in your spoken and written communications.

To reduce the excess words in your spoken communications, practice your most important messages out loud. The second time through is always better than the first, and the third time is better than the second.

Try to convey your entire point in one sentence. Maybe two.

Consider all the other "noise" that your audience, colleagues, and prospects are subjected to. They may already have listener fatigue before you start speaking. Be kind to them.

As I say to most of my clients when they're done speaking, "Now say it in half the words." It's a great exercise to reduce how much you say.

In your written communications, after creating a page or visual, take a moment to turn the page over, and then flip it once more to see it with fresh eyes. What's the first impression you have of the visual? Does the feeling of the imagery support the most important concept or message? Does it elevate your words, or distract from them?

Remember: half the words—twice the impact.

In the words of Forrest Gump, "That's all I have to say about that."

Benefit Language

For every meeting, you should start by agreeing with your team on the top three messages you want to convey to this client or prospect on this day.

Underpinning everything is that you will always strive to build rapport and trust, but you do want to land some key points.

As you practice these messages, bottom-lining them to their most powerful, succinct format, pay attention to how you articulate the benefits of each of these facts.

In sales terminology, we use the terms *features* and *benefits*. The features are the things that describe the object, product, or firm. The benefits are what the client will derive from each feature.

We've developed a habit of stopping short and only delivering features:

1. Our firm is global.
2. Our team has more than one hundred years of combined business expertise in the field.
3. We have been in this market for more than thirty years.
4. We have a fund for everyone.
5. We operate as one team.

Check your last presentation or pitch and find the messages that are universally delivered and much repeated. All of the above are still just features.

To start speaking about benefits, you need to complete the sentence, "What this means for you is …"

1. Because our firm is global, we can see worldwide trends. That means we can keep you updated on implications for your current portfolio, save you time because we'll have done the research for you, and help mitigate risk and increase your revenue.
2. Because our team has more than one hundred years of combined business expertise, we've handled good markets and rough markets. We will save you time on your decision-making when it's time to pivot.
3. Because we've been in this market for more than thirty years, we have a name for being the best in the business,

which gives you security that we'll do it right (and maybe bragging rights!). It also means that you'll get the benefit of our vision for what's going to happen in the future based on those past trends.

4. We have a fund for everyone. What that means to you is that we will spend a great deal of time understanding exactly what you're hoping to create in your portfolio. Your time with us will be well spent to help us determine a bespoke strategy that will give you security and revenue.
5. We operate as one team. That means we can plug into best practices around the world and throughout the company. You will gain the collective wisdom of everyone at the firm. We are actually incentivized based on how well we do as a group and how well we do for our clients.

Once you've checked that your language is now more benefit-rich, you should answer the question, "Why should I believe you?"

How can you prove that what you've said is true? You should draw on different kinds of evidence. Some choices are:

- facts,
- statistics,
- examples,
- case studies,
- analogies,
- testimonials (celebrities, industry experts, clients),
- hypothetical situations,
- demonstrations, and

- strong visuals.

Facts

The estimated population of the United States as of this writing is 341.9 million people as of June 20, 2025.[5]

Statistics

The population growth rate in the United States in 2024 was 0.98 percent. This was the largest year-over-year increase since 2000 and 2001. The world's population growth rate in 2024 was 0.91 percent.[6]

Example

This could be a concept or a physical item, for example, a car. "Look at this model; this is what we mean by custom detailing."

Or, as a concept, you might say, "We are very high-touch. For example, I call my clients every week to share my views on the market."

Case studies

You might cite a study by the *Harvard Business Review* on two hundred companies and their leadership practices. Or you might detail a bespoke financial structure that you devised for a portfolio company.

Analogies

Use words to create an unforgettable image or connection.

---

5 "Population," US Census Bureau, www.census.gov/topics/population.html.

6 Kristie Wilder, "US Population Grows at Fastest Pace in More Than Two Decades," www.census.gov/library/stories/2024/12/population-estimates.html.

"Just as a car needs regular maintenance to function efficiently, a business needs consistent investment in employee training to remain competitive."

Testimonials

You can use client testimonials, industry experts, or celebrity testimonials.

Celebrity testimonial: "Serena Williams endorses Nike, citing its quality and performance for professional athletes."

Industry expert testimonial: "Dr. Jane Doe, a renowned dietitian, recommends this supplement based on its proven health benefits."

Client testimonial: "A client shared the following: 'After using this software, our sales increased by 30 percent in just three months.'"

Hypothetical situations

"Imagine you're walking into a room and instantly feeling relaxed because of a calming fragrance. That's the kind of experience our essential oils create."

Demonstrations

You might give a tour of your company and say, "As you walk on our factory floor, you will note how everyone here is engaged in safety practices."

I often remind my clients that the meeting you're having with your prospect or client is a demonstration of what it feels like to work with you!

Strong visuals

A picture is worth a thousand words. What can you inspire by showing a beautiful photograph or a visual rendering?

One of my clients once included a picture of a worker sitting alone on a steel beam, high up in the air with the ground far below him. You immediately felt the height and precariousness of his "workplace." Then my client started to talk about the importance of safety gear, and the audience was fully attuned to his message.

Of course, we see a lot of charts and maps in presentations. Look for one that tells the story more succinctly than you can. "You see that arrow pointing dramatically up and to the right? That was our profit after we implemented this process."

I am not suggesting that you use all of these types of evidence. That would overwhelm your client. You should pick and choose which type of evidence best suits the individuals you are speaking with in each situation. It's great to prepare something in every genre and then pick and choose according to the conversation and the questions you receive.

How will you know that you've provided the right measure of proof? Your decision-maker will be the judge of that!

On Robert Cialdini: Persuasion and Influence

"A well-known principle of human behavior says that when we ask someone to do us a favor, we will be more successful if we provide a reason. People simply like to have reasons for what they do."—Robert B. Cialdini, *Influence: The Psychology of Persuasion*

How do you get people to listen to what you have to say, whether or not you have authority or a title? The psychology of persuasion is a field that explores how individuals can influence and change the attitudes, beliefs, and behaviors of others. I recommend the work of Robert Cialdini. His groundbreaking book *Influence: The Psychology of Persuasion* is widely considered a seminal work in this area, revealing key principles that shape human behavior and decision-making.

Cialdini outlines the concepts of pre-persuasion and the tools of influence based on our innate reactions to the world, which can help you make your listener more receptive to your message.

Here is a summary of the tools of influence:

Reciprocity: People return favors. If you do something for somebody, they will feel obliged to do something for you, or they will at least feel better about doing something for you.

In the context of fundraising, reciprocity can be interpreted as "Give us your money, and we'll give you even more money back at the end of the investment." But it can also mean, "We will keep you informed on the turns of the market and what it means for your overall investing, and for that, we'd like your loyalty."

Reciprocity insight: A 1971 study by Regan found that participants were more likely to return a favor (buying raffle tickets) when someone had previously done them a favor (e.g., giving them a can of Coca-Cola), highlighting the effectiveness of the reciprocity principle in influencing behavior. [7]

Commitment and Consistency: People respond to others who are consistent in their messages. If you are constantly giving the same messages to people and acting in a consistent way, they will respond positively.

When people initially commit to something, they are more likely to follow through. Persuasion tactics often involve getting someone to make a small commitment, which then leads to larger commitments.

I remember going through sales training when I was a young banker. The facilitators taught the technique of asking the client to sign three times before closing a deal. The idea was that each incremental ask was larger than the one before. Think of a car dealer: "Do

---

7 Dennis T. Regan, "Effects of a Favor and Liking on Compliance," *Journal of Experimental Social Psychology* 7, no. 6 (1971): 627–639.

you want the heated seats? Sign here." "How about tire/wheel protection? Sign here." "Why not spring for the limited-edition model? Sign here."

This always struck me as too manipulative and overt. Yet, we are wired to stand by what we publicly commit to do. This explains the concept of a twelve-step program in which public commitment to staying sober is a key element. Similarly, once a client commits to a relationship with you, no matter how small, the chances increase that they will continue to work with you in the future.

Commitment insight: A 1966 experiment by Freedman and Fraser demonstrated that individuals who agreed to a small request (putting a sign in their window) were more likely to comply with a larger request (placing a large sign on their lawn), showcasing the power of small commitments in building up to bigger ones.[8] They coined this the foot-in-the-door technique.

Social proof: If people see others doing something, they assume that it must be OK to do it, and, therefore, they will be happier about doing it themselves. People tend to follow the actions of others, especially in uncertain situations. This principle suggests that we are more likely to do something if we see others doing it, which is why testimonials, reviews, and social media influencers are so effective in persuasion.

I think this is why the world of finance is so committed to the PowerPoint deck! Everyone's done it, and for so many years that it's become a bad habit.

Social proof insight: Research by Robert Cialdini himself revealed that people were more likely to litter when they saw others

8 Jonathan L. Freedman and Scott C. Fraser, "Compliance Without Pressure: The Foot-in-the-Door Technique," *Journal of Personality and Social Psychology* 4, no. 2 (1966): 195–202.

doing the same, illustrating how social behavior is influenced by the actions of others.[9]

Authority: We are more likely to be persuaded by individuals who appear to be experts or have authority in a given field. This principle underscores the power of credentials, titles, and perceived expertise in influencing others.

Authority insight: Authority can be used to good and bad effect. It's important to focus on genuineness, transparency, and ethics. Employed well, authority can create strong bonds of influence and leadership; when applied poorly, it can lead to distrust and resistance.

Liking: People are more easily persuaded by those they like and who share similarities with them. Building rapport and fostering positive relationships are powerful tools of persuasion.

The esteemed firm Kohlberg Kravis Roberts & Co. has built its business with the firmwide belief that "people do business with people they like and trust."[10] This phrase was coined by Henry Kravis and George Roberts when they started the firm. It has become so fundamental to how the firm approaches its client relationships that I believe it's one of the key elements to its ability to maintain such a strong culture through expansion and growth. The company is grounded in the respect that colleagues have for their clients and for each other.

Liking insight: Research by Byrne, London, and Griffith (1968) demonstrated that people are more likely to be persuaded by indi-

---

9 Robert B. Cialdini et al., "A Focus Theory of Normative Conduct: Recycling the Concept of Norms to Reduce Littering in Public Places," *Journal of Personality and Social Psychology* 58, no. 6 (1990): 1,015–1,026.

10 *Mastering Private Equity* by Michael Prahl, Claudia Zeisberger, and Bowen White features a foreword by Henry Kravis, who notes, "As we work to build strong relationships with our stakeholders, we remember: 'People do business with people they like and trust.'" This underscores the importance of building strong relationships with stakeholders in private equity.

viduals whom they find to be similar to themselves, emphasizing the importance of common ground and empathy in persuasion.[11]

Scarcity: The perception that something is limited or in short supply can drive people to act quickly. This principle is often used in marketing strategies (e.g., limited-time offers, "while supplies last" promotions) to create urgency.

"When our freedom to have something is limited, the item becomes less available, and we experience an increased desire for it. However, we rarely recognize that psychological reactance has caused us to want the item more; all we know is that we want it. Still, we need to make sense of our desire for the item, so we begin to assign it positive qualities to justify the desire." —Robert Cialdini

Scarcity insight: A study by Worchel, Lee, and Adewole (1975) showed that participants rated cookies more highly when there were fewer available, reinforcing the idea that perceived scarcity increases desirability and value.[12]

Overall, the psychology of persuasion is a powerful tool for influencing human behavior, and understanding its principles can lead to more effective communication, marketing, leadership, and negotiation strategies. The key to successful persuasion lies in utilizing these principles ethically, ensuring that they align with the values and needs of both the persuader and the audience.

11 Michael Bond et al., "Effect of Occupational Prestige and Attitude Similarity on Attraction as a Function of Assumed Similarity of Attitudes," *Psychological Reports* 23 (1968): 1,167–1,172.

12 Stephen Worchel, Jerry W. Lee, and Akanbi Adewole, "Effects of Supply and Demand on Ratings of Object Value," *Journal of Personality and Social Psychology* 32, no. 5 (1975): 906–914.

The Power of Metaphors and Analogies

When it comes to persuasion, the right analogy or metaphor can make a world of difference in how your message is received. Just like a good story can captivate an audience, well-chosen metaphors and analogies can take complex, abstract concepts and translate them into something that resonates with people on a personal level. These tools help your audience grasp unfamiliar ideas by connecting them to something they already understand—creating a bridge between the unknown and the known.

Metaphors and analogies are essential in business storytelling, especially when you need to simplify technical language or data. For example, when explaining a complicated financial strategy to a client, comparing it to a familiar process, such as the steps of cooking a recipe, makes the concept more relatable. "Just as you carefully measure your ingredients to ensure a successful dish, we will carefully balance your portfolio to achieve the best financial outcome." This metaphor helps the audience see the process in a more familiar, accessible way, making the information easier to understand and remember.

Additionally, metaphors and analogies aren't just for explaining—they can also strengthen your argument by making your message more memorable. A compelling metaphor can stay with your audience long after your presentation, making your points stick and driving your persuasive effort. For instance, if you're advocating for a change in company strategy, you might use a metaphor like "We're at a crossroads, and this decision will chart the course for our future growth" to illustrate the gravity of the decision.

But just like a good story, a metaphor or analogy needs to be appropriate to the context and audience. A metaphor that resonates with one group might fall flat with another. It's important to choose comparisons that align with your audience's experiences and values. For instance, while the cooking recipe analogy might work well with individuals who enjoy cooking, it might not have the same impact in a highly technical or scientific environment. Understanding your audience's background and interests is key to selecting the right metaphor or analogy that will elevate your message.

Incorporating metaphors and analogies into your business presentations can significantly boost your ability to persuade, clarify, and connect with your audience. They allow you to break down complex ideas, making them tangible and relatable while also creating a more engaging, impactful narrative.

7

TELLING THE STORY

"Great stories happen to those who can tell them."

—IRA GLASS

It's important to think about your communication as a good story. Have you ever been in a meeting that seemed to run on without end, where people said the same things over and over and nothing was accomplished? I've seen it happen where, at the end, long after the designated stop time for the meeting, someone rattled off, "Here's what we've agreed to," and there were sounds of disagreement and dissent: "No! That's not what we said at all …"

A lot of words and wasted time.

Many years ago, someone asked about my role at the bank.

I said, "I am a professional meeting attender. I attend meetings all day long where we talk about really important and pressing problems and then have no time left in the day to take any action."

I felt such a sense of futility!

Peter Rogen once defined communication as "an exchange of energy, ideas, and emotions, between two people, that is received and understood."[13]

What resonated the most for me was the concept that communication, no matter how beautifully delivered, was meaningless unless it was *received and understood.*

---

13 Rogen Presentation Skills training manual, circa 1997.

That's why it's so important to make our messages clear and uncomplicated. And it's important to borrow what we know about telling and hearing stories. They teach us many important truths, and stories can be fun, memorable, scary, or exciting.

Keep in mind, as we noted at the beginning of this book, every good story has a beginning, a middle, and an end. This concept was originally defined by Aristotle. The beginning sets the context, the middle is where we hear all the details, and the end tells us what to think about what we've just heard.

OK, so that's great for Aristotle, but how do you incorporate this concept of beginning, middle, and end into a business presentation? You follow a simple format.

Structuring the Message

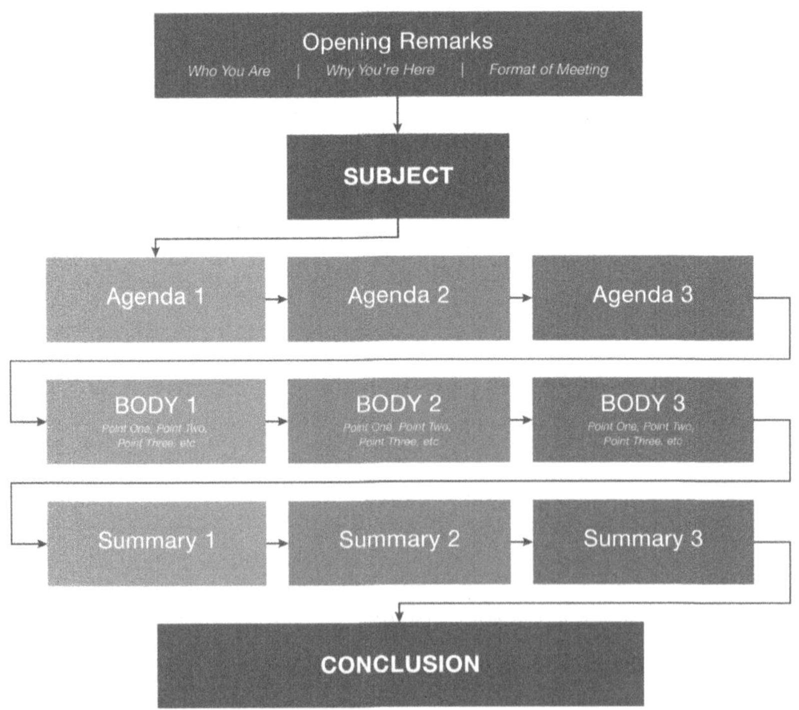

Source: CCB Communications, LLC.

Opening Remarks

You're sitting in the audience, waiting for a presentation to start.

Someone walks on stage. You notice whether they stride confidently to the center of the stage or stand awkwardly in the corner. They pause for a moment before they start speaking, and then they welcome you, the audience, to the event.

They tell you who they are, what the agenda for the program is, and who will be speaking, and they may even give you a hint as to what their objective for the meeting/day/conference might be.

They share an agenda for the event, tell you what time lunch will be served, and may even highlight any other dignitaries or guest speakers. And then they say, "And now to begin …"

Now, imagine you are that speaker, standing on a stage, alone. There are spotlights beaming at you, and there is an auditorium of people waiting for you to begin speaking. An inner voice may ask, "Are they going to like my presentation? Are they even going to care?"

The answer is yes, if you make them curious to learn more from you.

When you start a presentation, we recommend that you first clear any clutter from your audience's mind. Introduce yourself, advise your audience to either ask questions throughout or hold questions until the end, and give an expectation of the amount of time the presentation will last. Housekeeping. Now, they will have space in their minds for new ideas.

This moment gives the audience time to adjust to your energy, style, and presence. It should clear their minds of any distractions and help them get ready to listen.

But how do you make them lean forward in anticipation immediately after this?

You might consider a creative opening. This is when most people say, "Oh, you mean a joke."

The Creative Opening

Humor is wonderful to include in any presentation but be wary of telling a joke. There are very few really great joke tellers. There are even fewer politically correct jokes. Try a funny anecdote or observation instead. Try to use something that won't offend anyone. In other words, go carefully.

I think a better way to insert humor is through an anecdote or witty response. But we're not limited to humor. We can also spark interest in what is to come with a demonstration or a rhetorical question.

I recently did a program on executive presence. It's my habit to try to greet participants when they enter a room, shake their hand, and introduce myself. I find it creates an immediate connection.

I started my program by saying, "Today, we're going to talk about executive presence. To that end, I watched each of you enter the room. Do you want to know my first impressions of you?" That got their attention.

There are so many variations on this theme!

Start with a provocative question: "What if I could guarantee you'll get promoted in one year's time?"

When you ask a question, everyone in the audience immediately tries to answer it—not out loud, but in their minds. You have just started a conversation, and now you have a better chance of keeping their attention.

A famous example of a great creative opening was done by model Cameron Russell in her 2012 TED Talk about her modeling career. She walked onstage in a little black dress, then took a moment to change her clothes onstage, pulling on a long skirt, adding a comfy

Ideas for a Creative Opening

- Display a powerful image: a photograph or a drawing that depicts a place, concept, or idea visually.
- Consider using a prop, such as holding up a small medical device that fits in the palm of your hand and explaining that it is responsible for saving thousands of lives a year.
- Offer a personal tale: Those of you who know my story of how I broke both my arms in 2023 can imagine my walking onstage holding a small paddle and starting a talk with, "I want you to consider that pickleball can be dangerous to your health."
- Create a story that starts with "Imagine that ..."
- Challenge the audience: "You might believe xyz ... but what if I told you ..."
- Share a quote or a surprising statistic.
- Play music or a video clip.
- Do something unexpected but relevant.

sweater over her head and switching into comfortable shoes. It was a perfect setup for her discussion on "Looks Aren't Everything."

This example illustrates the critical importance of connecting your creative opening to your topic.

In order for your opening to succeed, it has to correlate with the ending. The key to a strong presentation is ensuring consistency between your opening, tone, and main message. That's why it's often best to craft your opening after you've defined your conclusion. Your opening should serve as a preview, setting the stage for the ideas you'll fully develop later on.

The Subject

I know it sounds silly, but it's important to notify your listeners that you're talking about something specific! You can wordsmith the phrasing depending on the dominant SOCIAL STYLE® of your decision-maker.

It's important to put it out there. "I'm here to speak about *this*." The subtext is, I want you to do this or to think that, and I want you to feel great about me as the messenger.

The Agenda

I find that some people are lost without an agenda. Others prefer to make it up as they go along. I'm in the camp that an agenda is your road map that starts your journey off in the right direction: We're going to go straight, take a right, then a left, and then continue onward …

The trick is to list the topics that you are going to address without jumping immediately into the details. The agenda is directional.

My clients know that I always suggest pausing after an agenda to inquire, "Is that the right order?" This allows your audience to say, "I would prefer we talk about agenda item three first" or "I'm not interested in agenda item two." It helps you tailor the message to their needs, not yours. With this structure, it's an easy thing to mentally move a column and stay on track.

I have written three agenda boxes on the page. You are not limited to three; your subject may require four or five. But there is a magic to grouping items in threes.

The magic of three refers to the psychological phenomenon whereby people tend to remember information better when presented in sets of three, often called the rule of three; this is because our brains naturally seek patterns, and three is the minimum number needed to form a recognizable pattern, making it easier to process and retain information compared to larger sets.

Key points about the magic of three:

Pattern recognition: Our brains are wired to identify patterns, and three items create a basic, easily recognizable pattern.

Cognitive efficiency: Breaking information into threes allows for easier processing and storage in memory.

Cultural influence: The number three has long been associated with completeness and perfection in many cultures, reinforcing its memorability.

Examples of the magic of three in practice:

- Slogans and phrases: "Life, Liberty, and the Pursuit of Happiness" from the Declaration of Independence
- Storytelling structure: A story typically has a beginning, middle, and end.
- Persuasive speeches: Effective speakers often present key points in threes to enhance memorability.
- Marketing and design: Companies often highlight three key features of a product to make it easier for customers to remember.

Just remember, it's as simple as one, two, and three.

The Body of the Presentation

When you are done with the agenda, you transition to the body section. This is the longest part of the presentation. Each body correlates with a separate agenda item, and you deliver them in that order: body one to body two to body three. They are not necessarily the same length, or even of the same importance. The body will contain the details, the facts, the anecdotes, and the persuasive arguments. If one of the topics requires a lot of talking or detail, you might even end the body section with a mini summary to anchor the message. Then you transition to the next body.

And so forth.

When you are done with the third—or final—body section, you transition to the two-part close:

The Summary and the Conclusion

The summary for each section is the one-sentence, most important message of all the things you've already said; there is no *new* news in a summary. It's as if you're saying, "Of all the things I told you in body one, remember this," and "Of all the things I told you in body two, remember this," and finally, "Of all the things I told you in body three, remember this …"

Told quickly and in a run, a good summary line will give you liftoff for the conclusion, the bow on the package, the last thing you will say. A conclusion should not be, "Are there any questions?"

It should be, "Here's what you should do, think, or feel as a result of what we just discussed."

I'll share an example with you, labeling these various elements (subject, agenda, and so on) I employ when I take the stage to give a demonstration of a presentation.

Opening Remarks

"My name is Cathy Bonczek, but you can call me Coach Cathy. I'm going to speak for about four minutes. Please hold your questions until the end of the presentation because we'll still have some time together."

The Subject

"I skipped breakfast today, and I'm feeling a little low energy at the moment. When that happens, I think about what I can do as a pick-me-up. My solution is always the same: Eat a piece of fruit. So, I am going to share my thoughts about my three favorite fruits."

The Agenda

"They are apples, oranges, and bananas."

At this point, I stop and ask the audience, "Do you like these three fruits?" I get lots of yeses and the occasional "What about kiwis?" Then I ask, "Is this the right order of preference?" We negotiate for a bit, and often, I agree to change the order to, say, bananas or oranges first, depending on the crowd.

Transition

"So let me begin by telling you why I like apples."

Body 1

"I like apples because I am an English major. (*This always generates a reaction—a chortle or a look of, 'What is she talking about?'*) That may not make sense to you, but I challenge you to go into a grocery store and read the names of the apple varieties. They are fantastic!

"There's Pink Lady. I imagine I have to wear a pink ruffled shirt to eat this apple. There's Fuji. I have to travel to Japan. There's McIntosh. Think men in kilts. And one can make up a whole romance about a Pink Lady and a McIntosh man in neighboring orchards. There's Honeycrisp; that just sounds wonderful. And, if you are anyone other than Snow White, how could you refuse someone offering you something called a Red Delicious? The name says it all."

I often insert a story here about my being a Cornell graduate and how the Cornell orchards make a new variety of apple every year. I share my quest to find a SnapDragon apple and how I've learned it's now mainstream and is the official apple of the Buffalo Bills.

"So yes, the names of apples get my innate storyteller going, but what do we know about apples? They are full of fiber and nutrients. If you eat an apple a day… *(I always pause here because every audience chimes in with, 'You keep the doctor away.')*

"We can all agree that apples are a lot of fun and good for you."

Transition

"But what about my second favorite fruit, the orange?"

Body 2

"I call oranges 'portable sunshine.' You can take an orange, throw it into your briefcase, and its thick skin protects your papers and laptop from the juice. I'm often working in New York City, and after walking through the canyons of buildings and settling into a client's conference room, I will pull out my beautiful orange globe for a refreshing break.

"I look at the beautiful round object and reflect, *Sunshine made this.*

"I will peel back the skin and sometimes get a little squirt of juice in my eye as the room fills with the citrus scent. It's a wonderful sensory moment.

"Then I eat the juicy sections and feel rejuvenated. I know, too, that I am getting a dose of vitamin C that will help bolster my immune system and keep me healthy.

"So, the orange represents a simple moment of color, sunshine, and health."

Transition

"Which leads us to the third and final fruit, the banana."

Body 3

"I first discovered I liked bananas as a little girl. Bananas were a main ingredient in banana splits. Who wouldn't love something that came with ice cream, caramel, chocolate, and whipped cream?

"But if you eat a lot of banana splits, you may gain weight. I did. As an adult, I went to WeightWatchers and they said, 'You can't eat the whole banana; it's too caloric!' You must cut it in half and consider it as TWO fruits.

"However, as I continued to explore ways to keep healthy, I started to work out more. When you work out your muscles, you need to replenish your potassium. Guess what? Bananas have potassium!

"This knowledge gave me a way to work bananas back into my life in a healthier way."

Transition

"What we've seen today is …"

Summary on 1, 2, and 3

"An apple a day will keep the doctor away, the portable sunshine orange will give you a good dose of vitamin C, and the forbidden fruit contains potassium and is actually good for your muscles."

Conclusion

"If you haven't yet had enough fruit today, I urge you to have a fruit salad at lunch!"

When I am done, the audience often tells me variations of the following:

"You were so relaxed. You were just talking to us."

"I can repeat your summary and conclusion, and I remember everything you said."

"You must really love apples …"

Last week, I gave this sample presentation to a client I was coaching. We were on Zoom, and I had clicked on the AI companion to capture notes as we were talking. After we were done, the AI notetaker sent me the recap. I laughed out loud when the notes said, "Cathy and Jack engaged in a conversation about fruit." I was delighted that the AI bot perceived it to be a two-way conversation and not just a speech/presentation or one-way delivery.

Become a Storyteller

Storytelling isn't just for novels and movies; it's a powerful tool in business, particularly when it comes to presenting data. While numbers and facts are important, they only become meaningful when woven into a compelling narrative. Just as every good story has a beginning, middle, and end, your data should be framed within a structure that makes it accessible and memorable for your audience.

The key to successful storytelling with data is making it clear and uncomplicated. Like any good narrative, you need to set the context, provide the details, and close with a conclusion that drives home the key message. For instance, imagine you're presenting sales figures or performance metrics. Instead of dumping a slide full of numbers, you could start by setting the stage: "Over the past quarter, our company has faced significant challenges, but these numbers tell a story of resilience and growth." From there, you walk the audience through the details, the middle part of the story, showing how each data point contributes to the larger narrative. Finally, you close by driving home the main takeaway: "Despite obstacles, we've grown 20 percent, and we're on track to exceed targets in the coming quarter."

This structure mirrors the classic storytelling arc: The beginning sets the context and the problem, the middle provides the journey, and the end delivers the resolution and calls to action. By framing your data within this narrative structure, you ensure your audience not only understands the information but is also engaged by it.

Incorporating visuals into your storytelling can further enhance this process. Think of your slides as scenes in a movie; each slide should move the narrative forward, adding depth to the story without overwhelming the audience with too much information. Use charts, graphs, and images to emphasize key points, but keep them simple and aligned with the story you are telling.

The key to successful persuasion through storytelling with data is emotional engagement. Just as a great story pulls at our emotions, effective data presentations should connect with the audience on a deeper level. By framing your data in a way that resonates with your audience's values, concerns, and goals, you can turn dry numbers into compelling stories that drive action.

Storytelling with data is not about presenting facts in isolation—it's about crafting a narrative that brings those facts to life. By following the tried-and-true structure of storytelling and making your message relatable, you can ensure that your data is not only understood but remembered.

Connect to Core Values

In addition to the structure of your story, a key element to crafting a persuasive presentation is connecting your message to the core values of your audience. Understanding what matters most to your listeners—whether it's their goals, aspirations, or concerns—allows you to tailor your narrative in a way that resonates deeply with them. By weaving these values into your story, you create an emotional connection that not only engages your audience but also strengthens the impact of your message. Linking your data or key points to the values your audience holds dear makes your presentation both informative and compelling.

This became very clear to me at a certain point in my own life.

Nine years ago, I was diagnosed with stage 4 chronic lymphocytic leukemia, and I was given a prognosis of approximately ten years to live. At the same time, my eldest son needed to change schools. He was leaving his private school and entering the public school system as he started high school. Since my son has dyslexia, he needed some accommodations at school. Normally, you meet with the school administrators, but because he hadn't yet started high school, the meeting was arranged with the middle school teachers.

I went into the meeting, accompanied by our family lawyer and school advocate, determined to set my son up for success. I was aware that the people I was meeting for the first time would then, in turn, have to persuade the high school team to support my child.

I told the administrators our journey through infertility and adoption: the story of how my son came to be my son. I added details about the struggles he'd had in school in his earlier years. I shared with them the news of my own precarious health and charged them with the care of my son, in the case that I wouldn't be there to do it for and with him.

Everyone at the table was crying by the time I was done. I was, too. I was simply sharing my profoundest hopes and fears. They rallied and helped put together a request for accommodations that would bolster my son in his future years.

When we left the building, my lawyer turned to me and said, "I want to be you when I grow up."

She asked me how I did it. I replied, "I just told our story."

Creating Emotional Engagement

In addition to structuring your story effectively, it's crucial to engage your audience emotionally. A well-told story doesn't just convey information; it stirs emotions that help your message resonate deeply. Whether you're presenting a business proposal, delivering a keynote, or pitching a new idea, crafting an emotional connection can transform your audience's experience from passive listening to active engagement.

To achieve this emotional connection, it's important to weave suspense, empathy, and excitement throughout your story, especially in the middle (the body), where the bulk of the content lies. These techniques will ensure your audience not only listens but also feels the message you're delivering.

Building suspense: Just like in a novel, suspense keeps your audience on the edge of their seats. You can build suspense by carefully pacing the delivery of your message, revealing key points gradually, and leaving certain questions unanswered until later. This makes the audience eager to find out what comes next, keeping them engaged. For example, in a business presentation, you could start by setting up the problem—something that feels urgent or unresolved—and then take the audience through the journey of how you plan to solve it, revealing the solution only at the peak of your narrative.

Creating empathy: Connecting emotionally with your audience often involves showing them how your story or message impacts real people. This could be through personal anecdotes, customer stories, or illustrations that highlight the human side of your topic. For instance, if you're talking about a new product, instead of just listing features, share a story about how it has changed someone's life or solved a pressing problem. When your audience sees themselves in your narrative, they'll feel more connected to your message and more likely to engage with it.

Generating excitement: A great story builds toward something exciting. This excitement isn't just about what will happen next; it's about making the audience feel anticipation and energy as you deliver your message. You can generate excitement by emphasizing the potential of what's to come, whether it's the future of your business, the success of your proposal, or the impact of your idea. By creating an atmosphere of possibility and potential, you leave your audience not only informed but also excited about what lies ahead.

By incorporating these elements—suspense, empathy, and excitement—you can craft a presentation, pitch, or speech that not only shares information but also touches the hearts and minds of your audience. When people are emotionally engaged, they remember your message more clearly and are more likely to take action on it.

The Role of Conflict

In traditional storytelling, conflict is often what keeps the audience hooked. It introduces tension, challenges the protagonist, and creates the drive for resolution. In business presentations, this concept can be adapted in a constructive way to make your message more relatable, engaging, and impactful.

In the context of a business story, conflict doesn't have to mean a struggle or disagreement. Instead, it can be the challenge your company or your client faces. Whether it's a market challenge, a specific problem with a product, or a shift in the industry, addressing these conflicts openly can make your story resonate with the audience. It makes the journey you're presenting more human and relatable.

When introducing conflict in your presentation, remember that it must be framed as a challenge with a potential solution. Your solution should be presented as the hero that overcomes the conflict, leading to a positive outcome. For example, if you're discussing a new product or service, you might highlight the specific pain points your audience faces and then explain how your offering addresses and resolves those issues.

Think of this approach as the "problem–solution" framework. You create an emotional connection with your audience by showcasing the challenges your company or client may have faced. They can see themselves in that struggle, and when you provide the solution, it feels like a resolution to their own issues.

This technique does more than just present information; it creates a dynamic narrative that keeps the audience engaged and invested in the outcome.

Encouraging Audience Participation

A great way to engage your audience is by prompting people to share their experiences or thoughts. Asking questions throughout the presentation not only invites participation but also ensures that the audience feels included in the story. For example, during a presentation on a new business strategy, you might ask, "How many of you have faced a similar challenge in your company?" This simple question invites reflection, making the audience an active part of the story.

You can also use audience participation to direct the flow of your presentation. By asking open-ended questions, you allow the audience to shape the narrative as it unfolds. This could involve asking for feedback on the points you've made or allowing the audience to vote on which direction the presentation should take next. By incorporating these interactive elements, you empower your audience to influence the content of the story, making it feel more personal and relevant to them.

It's a Conversation, Not a Presentation

Being flexible during your presentation is key to keeping your audience engaged. While you might have a structured narrative, adapting to real-time feedback can make the experience more impactful. Pay attention to body language, facial expressions, and verbal responses to gauge how well your message is being received. If the audience seems disengaged, you may need to adjust your tone, pacing, or the level of detail you're presenting.

For example, if you notice a few people nodding or actively writing down your points, this could be a sign that you're connecting with them. On the other hand, if you see confusion or a lack of eye contact, it may indicate that you need to clarify your points or alter your delivery. I often stop and say, "Does that make sense?" and my audience will happily comment on what's resonated so far, or they'll ask a question for clarification. This real-time responsiveness can create a more fluid and engaging narrative, one in which the audience feels like an integral part of the storytelling process.

Strategies for Engagement

To make sure your audience is actively participating, try these strategies:

- **Ask questions:** Open the floor to the audience for their input at various points during your presentation.
- **Poll the audience:** Use interactive tools or simple hand-raising to get a sense of what your audience thinks.
- **Share personal stories and ask for theirs:** Tell a relevant personal anecdote and invite the audience to share their own experiences. This creates relatability and fosters connection.

- **Watch for feedback cues:** Be mindful of audience body language and energy. If they seem disengaged, change the pace or ask a question to get them back into the story.

By weaving these interactive elements into your storytelling, you create a collaborative environment in which your audience is not just receiving information but actively engaging in the narrative. In addition, your content will resonate strongly and be memorable.

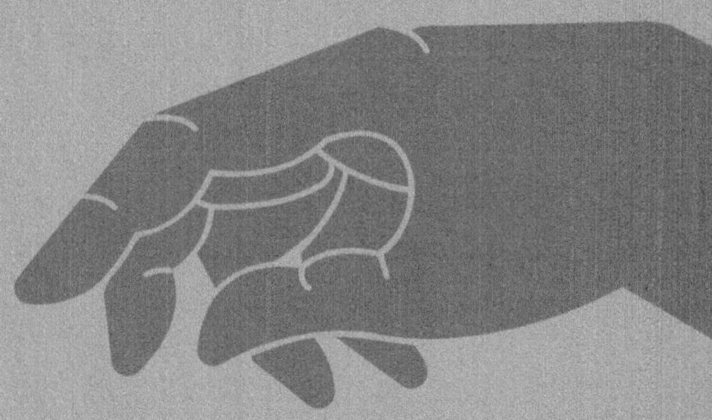

PART 2

PRACTICAL APPLICATION

8

OVERCOMING THE FEAR OF PUBLIC SPEAKING

"The only thing we have to fear is fear itself."

—FRANKLIN D. ROOSEVELT

Before there is a presentation, there is often fear.

We've all heard the maxim that people fear public speaking more than they fear death. If you are someone who gets nervous speaking in meetings, or if the idea of standing on a stage in front of an audience leaves you weak, it may help to know that you are not alone. In fact, glossophobia, the fear of public speaking, is said to affect 75 percent of the population.[14]

What may also help is knowing that there are many methods for working through stage fright or public speaking distress. Take some comfort in the knowledge that it's not always obvious when you are nervous, so if you can persevere and continue talking, there is a chance that everyone will perceive you as comfortable and competent.

It is important to start by assessing what's behind the fear. Ask yourself: What are you afraid of?

---

14 Ali Syed, PharmD, "Glossophobia: What Is It, Causes, Diagnosis, Treatment, and More," March 4, 2025, www.osmosis.org/answers/glossophobia.

1. Looking foolish?
2. Not knowing enough about the topic?
3. Getting a question that is challenging?
4. Making a mistake?
5. *Not being perfect?*

Once you've named the root of the problem, it is helpful to remind yourself that the potential consequences are fairly inconsequential in the grand scheme of a career. We are the ones who tend to catastrophize the idea of showing our flaws, when in fact, it is our flaws that make us endearing and authentic.

One of the most paralyzing aspects of public speaking is the belief that everyone is critically watching your every move. This common fear can cause speakers to become self-conscious and anxious, fearing that their every mistake will be noticed by the audience. However, the reality is often quite different. Audiences, more often than not, are focused on the content of the presentation and their own thoughts, not meticulously analyzing every aspect of the speaker's delivery.

Shifting from a mindset of "everyone is watching my every move" to "the audience is here to learn and engage with me" is a critical adjustment. When you focus on the message rather than on yourself, you free up mental space to engage more deeply with the audience and deliver your content effectively. In fact, studies have shown that audiences are generally less critical than speakers believe, and they are also more likely to be forgiving of minor mistakes.[15] Most audience members are preoccupied with processing information, reflecting on

---

15 S. B. Kaufman and D. R. Johnson, "The Psychology of Public Speaking: A Critical Overview," *Journal of Applied Psychology* 43, no. 2 (2018): 125–145.

their own experiences, or thinking about how the content applies to them, rather than scrutinizing the speaker's every gesture or word.

In addition to managing the internal anxiety and mindset discussed earlier, it's equally important to understand how your physical delivery can significantly impact your public speaking effectiveness. When we work with clients on their executive presence, we focus not only on the content of their presentation but also on the physical aspects of delivery—such as eye contact, gestures, movement, voice modulation, and pausing. These elements are often revelatory for many speakers because the focus in most businesses tends to be on the content itself, not the actual delivery of that content.

As you prepare to step in front of an audience, remember that how you present your message is just as important as the message itself. In fact, research shows that a strong, engaging delivery can enhance the clarity and impact of your message, making it more persuasive and memorable.[16]

For a deeper dive into how to master these physical elements of your presentation, we'll explore delivery skills in the next chapter, where we'll break down techniques for projecting confidence, engaging with your audience, and making sure your message lands effectively.

One way to combat the self-imposed pressure of perfectionism is by reframing the narrative around public speaking. Again, instead of viewing the audience as a critical group waiting for you to falter, see them as collaborators in the learning process. The focus should be on engagement rather than flawless delivery. When speakers accept that minor imperfections are natural and even relatable, they begin to create more authentic connections with their audience.

---

16 Alex B. Van Zant and Jonah Berger, "How the Voice Persuades," *Journal of Personality and Social Psychology* 118, no. 4 (2020): 661–682, https://doi.org/10.1037/pspi0000193.

Research in cognitive psychology supports this perspective. According to psychologist Jonathan Haidt, the human tendency to focus on perceived flaws is often exaggerated, and this tendency can be mitigated through cognitive reframing techniques such as visualization and positive affirmations.[17] Rather than fixating on potential flaws, speakers can reframe the experience as an opportunity to share valuable insights, ask for feedback, and engage in meaningful dialogue.

By focusing on the value you are providing to the audience, rather than fearing judgment, you transform the presentation into a collaborative, learning-focused experience. It's not about impressing people with perfection—it's about connecting with them through your authentic message.

We are often our own harshest critics when it comes to public speaking. We catastrophize the idea of showing any flaw, worrying that a small mistake will derail our entire presentation. However, as we noted, research shows that our flaws—what we consider imperfections—are often the very qualities that make us endearing, authentic, and relatable to our audiences.

Researchers Thomas Gilovich, Victoria Husted Medvec, and Kenneth Savitsky found that people tend to overestimate the impact of their actions in public settings. The spotlight effect suggests that we often think everyone is watching our every move, amplifying our fears.[18] The truth, however, is that our audience is far less focused on us than we think. In fact, audience members are typically more preoccupied with their own thoughts and concerns.

---

17 Jonathan Haidt, *The Happiness Hypothesis: Finding Modern Truth in Ancient Wisdom* (Basic Books, 2006).

18 Thomas Gilovich, Victoria Husted Medvec, and Kenneth Savitsky, "The Spotlight Effect in Social Judgment: An Egocentric Bias in Estimates of the Salience of One's Own Actions and Appearance," Journal of Personality and Social Psychology, 78, no. 2 (2000): 211–222.

A study by Gilbert et al. in 2002 found that individuals often catastrophize their mistakes in social situations, assuming that others are scrutinizing them.[19] Yet, in reality, the people around us are usually far less judgmental than we imagine. The "no one is watching you" concept—often cited in social media and self-help circles—reinforces this idea: The people in the audience are far more focused on themselves than on the potential flaws of the speaker.

Isolating this misconception is key to overcoming the fear of public speaking. When we allow ourselves to show our imperfections, we're allowing our authentic selves to shine through. And this authenticity is often what creates a stronger connection with the audience. People will remember your message because you were real, human, and relatable—not because you were flawless.

So, rather than catastrophizing the idea of making mistakes, try to embrace your imperfections. Instead of fearing that an awkward pause or a small slip will ruin your presentation, consider how that moment could make you more authentic and relatable. By accepting and even highlighting our flaws, we can build rapport and trust with our audience, turning those "mistakes" into moments of connection.

Next, try to recall: What happens when you get nervous?

1. You experience flop sweat.
2. Your voice becomes tremulous.
3. Your heart starts to pound.
4. Your hands shake.
5. Your brain shuts down.

---

19 Max Birchwood, Alan Meaden, Peter Trower, and Paul Gilbert, "Shame, humiliation, and entrapment in psychosis: A social rank theory approach to cognitive intervention with voices and delusions," in *Casebook of Cognitive Therapy for Psychosis*, ed. Anthony P. Morrison (Routledge, 2002), 108–131.

6. You start speed-train talking.
7. You keep adding words and create run-on sentences.
8. You become monosyllabic.
9. You turn bright red.

In some cases, public speaking can induce a panic attack, which is a more intense, even frightening, reaction. Once you've experienced that, the memory of a panic attack can be a trigger for another one when you are asked to speak in public again.

One of the most common barriers to overcoming the fear of public speaking is negative self-talk. You've probably experienced thoughts like, "I'm going to make a fool of myself" or "I'm not good enough for this presentation." These thoughts can snowball, paralyzing you with anxiety and making it harder to focus on the task at hand. The key is to challenge these irrational thoughts and replace them with rational ones.

Cognitive behavioral therapy techniques can be a game changer in managing these negative internal dialogues. For instance, when you catch yourself thinking, "I'm going to bomb this," you can challenge it by reminding yourself, "I have prepared well, and I am capable of handling this." This process of reframing allows you to shift from a mindset of fear and doubt to one of confidence and capability.

Visualization is another powerful technique. Picture yourself walking up to the stage with confidence, speaking clearly, and engaging the audience with ease. This mental exercise can trick your brain into believing that success is already within your reach. Combining this with positive affirmations, such as "I'm ready for this," can significantly reduce the fear and help foster a self-supporting mindset that propels you toward success.

You might also try journaling these thoughts before your presentation, writing down your anxieties and then countering them with facts about your preparation and past successes. Over time, this practice will help you develop a more rational and supportive internal dialogue.

Know that there are remedies for most of these events, ranging from carrying a handkerchief (to address the flop sweat) to taking a prescription drug to reduce nerves. Again, the more you understand what is likely to happen, the more you can proactively find the right remedy.

Disclaimer: It's important to note that while there are remedies for most of these events, it is essential to consult a healthcare professional before using any prescription medications or treatments. Always seek advice from a doctor or mental health professional for tailored solutions to managing anxiety or panic attacks.

So, what else can you do to help reduce the nerves and the reactions? Think of the four P's of gaining power and poise in public. (Did you see what I did there? I'm on an alliteration streak!)

Prepare.

1. Research your topic so you feel well versed.
2. Outline or write the structure of your remarks.
3. Visit the venue; walk on the stage before you have to present.
4. Craft a beautiful two-sentence conclusion that sums up the whole topic. This is your default "landing" if you run out of time or you forget everything else you have to say!

5. Choose visual aids that *actually aid* you (i.e., slides with a key word to prompt the main message, or notes that you can place on a nearby podium). Make sure your notes are written in a large font so that words can be easily picked up at a glance.
6. If you are someone prone to panic attacks, you may choose to take a calming medication to help.

Practice.

1. Proclaim yourself a victor. Visualize yourself finishing the presentation and receiving wild applause.
2. Rehearse the presentation in full, over and over again, so that you can deliver it in a conversational manner.
3. When time is short, rehearse the beginning and the end, the introduction and the conclusion. These are usually the most difficult moments of a meeting or presentation.
4. Ask trusted colleagues, friends, or family members to listen to the presentation.
5. Practice your power pose or stance to remind your brain and body that you have poise and control.
6. Practice pausing at the end of every statement. Elongate these moments of silence; they will make you seem confident, and you will use them to breathe in much-needed oxygen.
7. Rehearse the worst-case scenario. What would happen if you forgot all that you were supposed to say? Well, you

could walk to the podium where you've dropped a few notes, catch your breath, and start from there.

I often tell the story of how I once fell off a stage while doing a presentation—on presentation skills—to an audience of two hundred people. I backed up too far on a platform stage and just disappeared. I was working with a partner who made a wonderful, deadpan quip: "Cathy will be back in just a moment." Everyone laughed. I bounced back up, told everyone I was just fine, and kept on going. Needless to say, I was very embarrassed, but I forced myself to just go on. Later, we were told by several audience members that they thought we might have planned that moment to make a point that you can recover from anything!

Pivot.

1. Remember that audiences want you to succeed and are always rooting for you.
2. Take a deep breath in (count to four) and exhale for a longer count (eight beats). The longer exhale helps relax your whole body. Do this several times.
3. Trust your body—taking a few steps in one direction or the other can "unfreeze" you and help release nervous energy.
4. Reduce your "self-attention" that is making you self-conscious by shifting your focus to people in the audience. Ask them, "Does that make sense?" and wait for them to affirm. Dialogue is as much of a gift to them as it is to you.

Persevere.

Just keep going no matter what happens. People will remember how you ended, not a lost moment here or there!

1. Finally, I remind you to be kind to yourself. No one else expects you to be perfect. People seek connection. Most audiences prefer real, slightly flawed human interaction.
2. Speaking in front of other people can be an act of bravery. You should applaud yourself every time you do it.

9

ON ACTING

"An actor's job is to make the audience believe what they're seeing is real. The same goes for leaders: To be persuasive, you must make people believe in your message."

—MERYL STREEP

As a young girl, I was very shy. My mother used to joke that I observed everything in silence until I was five years old and then started talking in perfect sentences when I finally felt comfortable.

My years of silence taught me the power of observation. But it was my years dabbling in acting that gave me my versatility and voice.

I was always drawn to the stage. In first grade, I auditioned for a local production of *Oliver!* I still don't know how I mustered the courage to do an audition, but I really wanted to try. I was crushed when I didn't get a part in the play. I started to cry. My mother, driving me home from the school auditorium said, "You were very good, just very quiet. Perhaps they needed someone louder."

After that, I tried singing for a while, doing a solo performance for my parents when I was in fifth grade. I still remember standing in the school library. (Why were we singing in the library? I don't recall.) I sang the theme song from the movie *Love Story*. My mother—my most faithful fan—gave me feedback afterward. She said, "You were very committed, even if you weren't on key."

Undeterred, I still thought of myself as destined for the stage. I was cast in a showcase of scenes, featuring one from *Oliver!*—my second chance. The director, Frank, asked if I would play the part of Bill Sikes. We obviously had a shortage of male actors. I was stunned. The scene called for me to yell at Nancy and even break a table in fury on stage. I had to learn how to raise my voice and yell at someone, all while keeping my face and body facing forward enough so the audience could see me. At one point, I raised a fist and brought it down on the "table" —a flimsy contraption of legs and plywood top, causing the top to split and the legs to topple. I wasn't very good at breaking things, but I soon learned the enormous satisfaction that came from pounding on furniture. (No, I did not do reenactments at home.)

I was very uncomfortable, but the more I rehearsed, the more I found a way to be Bill.

It was very empowering to know I had that force of personality in me. I acted in high school productions, but I did not pursue acting while in college. I wanted to put all my energy into studying.

But in my early New York years, the theater pulled me back in. I did productions in Brooklyn Heights with the Heights Players and studied with the Ensemble Studio Theatre in Hell's Kitchen, all while pursuing my banking career. The acting allowed me to express every emotion, to figure out ways of physically moving to make an impression, and also how to share a spotlight with others. All of these have bolstered my business interactions.

So, what can business leaders learn from actors?

When we work with clients on their executive presence, we focus on the physical aspects of delivery: eye contact, gestures, movement, voice modulation, and pausing. This is often revelatory because the focus in most businesses is on the content of the presentation, not the actual delivery of the information.

It can be discomforting to suddenly have to think about how you are going to walk on a stage, hold your hands and/or a clicker, modulate your voice, look audience members in the eye, and stop center stage to pause and let your important information sink in.

That's when people will ask, "Isn't that acting?"

I always reply, "No, it isn't acting, but it does require some of the same techniques and skills as acting."

The difference between acting and presenting is that when you are acting, you are saying someone else's words, perhaps pretending to be an entirely different person. Your job as an actor is to feel what that person would feel and behave how that person would behave—and to do all that through the prism of your body, your voice, your eyes.

In business, or even in your everyday communication, your job is to clearly communicate concepts, ideas, instructions, or goals. It is important to make these communications interesting, actionable, and maybe even exciting for your colleagues or friends. How you deliver these messages matters, and that's where the acting techniques can help you.

My beloved former acting teacher, and second mother, Janet Sarno, used to tell me, "You can't act an emotion; you have to feel something first." If you really feel something, then the audience will, too.

As business communicators, we should attempt to become expert orators as much as we strive to be subject matter experts in our lines of business. So, how do we use acting skills to show up as authentically great presenters?

To that end, *think about your entrance*: Don't just shuffle into a meeting room; walk in boldly as if this is the only place in the world you want to be right now.

Greet everyone with eye contact and words; connect visually with the people around the table before you grab your seat.

Open your presentation with a practiced, calm, and dynamic voice. Enjoy the fact that all eyes will turn to you. In reality, if you are selling or fundraising, you are the most important element of the sale—not the product. Your prospects will want to trust you before they open their wallets.

When you say something, *honor the punctuation*. Pause when you come to the end of a sentence or thought and let your audience hear what you just said, maybe even react to it.

Use your arms and hands to emphasize a point or illustrate a concept—like charades. It will help you use energy positively, and it will create interest for your listener as well as move your voice.

Use structure or talking points to deliver your lines—the powerful and succinct key messages you most want your audience to remember.

Feel something—passion or optimism, pride or concern—and let that underpin your words.

Listen carefully to what your audience is saying, and observe what is not being said. Great actors and gifted improvisation artists really listen to each other and react accordingly; they don't just march through a script. That's good advice for any meeting or presentation.

In short, don't think of acting as an exercise of fakery. Think of it as a set of skills to bring a story and emotions to life. Do think of your presentations as something that can be enlivening, entertaining, and impactful.

Acting isn't just about delivering lines—it's about reacting to others. This principle is critical when applying acting techniques to business presentations. Just as an actor constantly responds to the environment, their fellow actors, and the emotional tone of a scene, you, as a presenter, need to be able to engage with the audience and adapt based on their feedback, body language, and reactions.

In the business context, this translates into being adaptable during meetings and presentations. Many presenters focus primarily on what they want to say, often memorizing scripts or relying on index cards, but effective communication is about being open to the flow of conversation and engaging with your audience in real time. The ability to listen actively to the audience—whether it's noticing body language cues, responding to questions, or adapting your message based on feedback—enhances the overall effectiveness of the presentation. By allowing the audience to interact with you, you create a dynamic and engaging experience rather than a one-sided delivery.

One of the most powerful tools you have in your presentation arsenal is improvisation. It's common for presenters to feel that every part of their message needs to be rehearsed and perfected, but the best presentations allow space for flexibility and crowd work. This doesn't mean you should throw away your notes or your plan entirely; rather, it's about being comfortable with the unpredictable nature of human interaction and being willing to adjust. For example, if you're speaking to an audience that's becoming disengaged, it may be helpful to shift your tone or introduce an interactive question to reengage them. If someone challenges your point, rather than defensively sticking to your script, embrace the opportunity to have a conversation and delve deeper into the topic.

Incorporating audience interaction into your presentation plan is crucial for two reasons: It keeps your audience engaged, and it allows you to adjust your message based on the real-time energy of the room. This flexibility not only makes your presentation feel more authentic, but it also makes you appear more confident and in control. Audience members want to feel heard, and when you allow them to influence the course of your presentation, you create a collaborative environment that feels more like a dialogue than a lecture.

Crowd work—whether through story, questions, or even adjusting your delivery to meet the needs of your audience—allows you to break down the barrier between you and your listeners, creating a more human and engaging experience. Think of it as a partnership.

The audience is there to help shape your message just as much as you are there to deliver it.

In Shakespeare's words, "All the world's a stage."

How would I sum up what we can take away from actors?

1. **Charisma can be learned.**

   Eye contact, attention, movement, and posture all contribute to how you display confidence.

2. **The body matters when delivering a message.**

   We need to know how to control our pace, movement, stance. People take in the whole of us when we are speaking—not just our words.

3. **You do better when you are healthy.**

   Getting enough sleep, exercising, and eating nourishing food will help you have energy, flex your voice, and think sharply.

4. **You can breathe life into words that you say over and over.**

   There are some things that must be said. Actors must say the words that the writer put on the page. They then imbue those words with meaning and intention. Business leaders often find themselves on the road delivering the same message over and over, introducing the firm or a product. How do you make it sound conversational and fresh? You might try saying it as if you were sitting across the table from your best friend.

5. **You don't have to say anything to get all eyes on you.**

   Being still or being quiet has a great deal of power. Your energy still exudes from you. The actor wants to contribute to every scene, whether they have dialogue or not. Often, they do this by silently reacting. Your presence at a board table matters.

6. **You have to be in the moment and sometimes improvise.**

   Really great actors listen to the other actors on the stage or in the scene. It's not about just saying words in turn. Sometimes, the words come out differently than what was scripted, and the other actors have to react and bring the scene back.

7. **Your voice conveys much of the emotion of the message.**

   Lullaby or scream? You can choose from everything in between. Why have we decided collectively that it's professional to be monotone and dry?

8. **Rehearsals are mission-critical to being prepared.**

   Rehearsals are the place where mistakes happen. Rehearsals are where happy accidents and experiments change everything. The best rehearsals are run with permission to fail, as well as permission to dazzle. Refinement comes after repetition. This is time well spent because it helps you ready yourself for the actual performance.

   Why do we, in business, expect ourselves to be perfect without this trial and error? Usually, this is simply a time-based decision—we don't have any extra minutes in the day. The time you spend amounts to the gains you'll make in mastery.

9. **Courage can be cultivated.**

   The more you act, the better you become. It's exactly the same in business. The more you speak up, the better you become. Feedback—both positive and constructive—helps the actor and business leader make changes and grow in skill.

   Walking onto a stage or onto a movie set can be very intimidating because all eyes are on you. Do it anyway.

The bottom line is that there are profound parallels between acting and leadership. From learning charisma to mastering body language, maintaining health, breathing life into repetitive messages, commanding attention through silence, staying present, and embracing improvisation—each lesson underscores the artistry and discipline required in both acting and business. Rehearsing with courage, embracing feedback, and stepping onto the stage despite the spotlight's intensity—all of these empower us to not only perform but to lead with authenticity, grace, and impact. Just as actors refine their craft through practice and resilience, so too can business leaders. Embrace the stage, for every moment offers an opportunity to shine.

I remember a time when I brought a banking colleague to an external business meeting to introduce him to a client of mine that he thought was a good prospect for his product. We walked into the room where four men were waiting for us. There were only five chairs in the room. Everyone shook hands, and it was then suggested, rather rudely, that I was no longer needed in the room. I was walked to the door and ushered out.

I was enraged, as you can imagine. I took a moment and calmly introduced myself to the entire administration team. Then I used my acting skills to bolster my wounded pride. I adopted the posture of an extremely confident person. I grabbed a chair from the reception area, opened the closed door to the meeting room, dragged the chair in, and sat down in the middle of the men. I don't remember contributing much verbally to the conversation, but everyone was very aware of my presence. It had been a pretty spectacular entrance.

And that colleague never closed a door on me again.

10

DELIVERY SKILLS

"I speak two languages, Body and English."

—MAE WEST

There is a great tie-in between the acting techniques of using your hands and body and the building of executive presence.

I was recently running a group talk on executive presence. It was being held over Zoom, and as I was midsentence, my computer shut off, and I was bumped from the session. I hastily plugged in another laptop, hit the link, and rejoined the meeting, which reminded me that the first rule of executive presence is to be in the room!

But in all seriousness, that's what executive presence is all about—commanding space and respect. I always ask clients, "What is executive presence?" Here are some answers I receive:

"Perceived wisdom."

"The look of being in charge."

"Charisma."

"Experience."

"Someone who has executive presence makes you lean in to listen to them."

I also ask them, "What is gravitas?"

Most look puzzled and say, "It's executive presence …"

Gravitas means a solemnity or dignity of manner. It has the connotation of weightiness. How do you add these two components to your bearing? In order to augment your executive presence, consider the following.

Know what you stand for and what you want the world to see. Return to the five words you would use to define the "you" that you want your colleagues to see. Are you intelligent, creative, honest, brave, and a subject matter expert? Or, are you a visionary, charismatic, risk-taking, market-leading innovator?

What we think of ourselves shows in the way we hold our bodies. It's not just about having good posture, with shoulders back, head up high, striding into the room. It's about being comfortable standing in the limelight and saying to the people around you, "I am this …"

You can exude confidence before you feel it by mimicking the indicators: strong eye contact, firm voice, and standing tall in your boots. And when your confidence increases to match your outward appearance, others can feel it, too. It pulls people in. People are drawn to power.

You must engage. You don't have to say a lot, but you do have to say something. At work, you are responsible for offering an opinion and engaging. Having an amazing presence without saying a word is possible, but it's not the best strategy for a business career. Executive presence is a combination of physical attributes plus wisdom, experience, and added value. What you say should matter.

In order to make that so, when you speak, make sure you address the people in the room and articulate the relevance to them, specifically. Keep your remarks crisp and on point. There's something commanding about being able to sum up a complex situation in a few powerful words.

Gaining Gravitas

Since gravitas means weightiness, I suggest to my clients that slowing down their pace and their movements will add dignity.

There is an old Francis Ford Coppola movie called *Peggy Sue Got Married*. It was made in 1986, and it starred Kathleen Turner as a woman who, through some magic, returns to her high school days. Kathleen Turner's acting in the film is an amazing example of conveying youth or maturity through body language. She starts the film as her adult self, and her movements are measured and a bit weary. When she is acting as her sixteen-year-old self, she moves quickly, darting her head from side to side when listening to people and practically bouncing with energy.

In business, if you want to add weight to a thought or recommendation, you might slow down as you speak about it and be deliberate in telling the details. If you want to convey the energy and creativity of your big idea, speed up your speech, use your gestures to add energy, and put some "youth" into the idea.

Your silence is important. Deliberation is a component of gravitas. It adds formality. A well-placed pause will make people linger on the last thing you said, and the moment will invite them to react, interject, and converse. You must create moments of quiet in order for them to lean in a little closer to hear you.

You can acquire confidence, poise, and the ability to deliver crisp commentary even if you don't have these skills now. You rehearse to converse. Try using a louder voice than usual when you practice a presentation. Film yourself talking or giving a little speech, then watch and learn about your own body language. When delivering a message, halve the words and articulate the impact of your message, not the contextual details.

You must be *you*. The way in which I exude presence will be different from the way you do. The French have an expression, "*être bien dans sa peau*," which means to be comfortable in one's own skin. No one else can inhabit all the intricacies and elements that make you who you are.

Delivery Skills and the Seven Observables

Eye Contact and Facial Expression

When you start to talk about creating executive presence and gravitas, it's important to think about the delivery skills. There are seven categories that people observe about you when they first meet you, and these are the things you can use as a guideline to work on; they include eye contact and facial expression, voice, gestures, posture, movement, language, and dress.

Now, out of all of these, my experience has shown that eye contact is the single most important one. When eye contact is used well, the positive results can be numerous: People believe you're telling the truth, and that you're confident, trustworthy, charismatic, in charge, intelligent, dynamic, and strong. When eye contact is poor, all the opposite perceptions are possible: People could perceive that you're dishonest, lying, nervous, untrustworthy, out of control, not knowledgeable, boring, or weak. No one wants to convey all of that. So being able to connect with people in this way is very important.

I always say that when you don't know somebody's rank or importance in a meeting, you give them equal eye contact, and that could be something you have to get used to as well. Some people find making eye contact easy, while some find it more challenging. When you're looking at someone, you can always shift your focus from iris to iris so that you're focusing on their eyes. You get a sense of movement, and it also allows you to stay connected with them.

Try holding their eyes when you're looking for a thought rather than looking up or looking down. Look them in the eyes and just pause while holding eye contact. They'll know you're coming back to them and will stay connected to you. Simply speak when your thought comes to you.

The way you wield your eye contact can make you seem dominant and challenging or gentle and deferential. When in doubt, give an equal amount of eye contact to the amount you are receiving.

In addition to helping your brand and conveying your strength and your connection, eye contact has another really important value. That is, when you are looking at someone's eyes, you can't help but see their face. As you start paying attention to people's faces, you'll see the microexpressions, the furrowed brows, the pouted lips, the quizzical jaunt of the eyebrow.

All of these are how people communicate with you nonverbally. That wealth of information is wonderful for you whenever you're presenting, speaking, or engaging others in a meeting. It allows you to react, pivot, ask a question, inquire, or explore what the expression means. That level of attention to your audience is a wonderful way to help build rapport. It's also a demonstration of the kind of care you'll show them if they should partner with you. When you think about it, you have a lot of power to affect your audience through the simple means of how you look at them.

Voice

Your voice is the soundtrack to your movie or story. Taking care to use the right vocal modulation, volume, pacing, and projection is a key component in the interest and emotion you'll create. Then, there's the power of the pause.

As I mentioned earlier in the book, I started studying voice when I was in middle school so I could sing in my school choir. I learned relative pitch. I learned how to hit the right notes. I've learned how the rests make music and how those pause moments add artistry and dimension to a song. I learned that breath is critical to making sound and calming nerves.

I also learned the importance of placing the right notations on your sheet music to give your brain a shortcut to knowing what to do next. There is technique in glancing at your sheet music but keeping your head lifted so your voice will carry and you can keep your eyes on the conductor, who is setting the pace for you and the orchestra.

I learned the importance of projection, how to have your voice carry into the room and reach your intended audience. I learned that articulation is important so that the words you are singing are understandable.

Finally, there was the realization that all notes are not created equally and that dynamics (modulation) are key to setting the mood of the piece.

I believe these aspects of voice are underutilized in our corporate meetings and boardrooms. We've gotten into a habit of using a very narrow bandwidth of volume because it's acceptable and we try not to bring too much drama into our workdays. I think this is a slight mistake.

Some words and sentences are more important than others. Knowing how to create an uplift or an increase in volume to add momentum or switching to your dulcet tones to convey bad news should be part of your technique.

How can you use all the nuance of your voice in a Zoom meeting?

Start by signing in to your Zoom meetings early. Ask a trusted colleague to join you and do a sound check. Can you be heard? Is the quality crisp? What's the tone of your voice? How loud is the volume?

All of these things will impact the perception that your clients have of you.

Perhaps you're speaking in your second or third language and are concerned some listeners will have a hard time understanding your accent. Slowing down and using judicious pauses after certain words will help your audience with comprehension.

Practice the pause. When you rehearse, it's a good idea to exaggerate the pauses. I sometimes tell my clients, "When you come to a period or a comma, do a quick one, two, three count before you move on."

Your audience understands what you just said in the silence. The pause will invite them to think for a moment on your comment, reflect, and maybe even comment. Don't rush past these wonderful moments of comprehension.

There's another benefit to effective pausing. Once you start to slow down and use the spaces between the words more wisely, you will see a reduction in filler words. Those are the sounds we make such as "uh," "you know," "kinda," "sort of," and "right." Often, these noises are there because you're trying to have your mouth keep pace with your brain. Take a moment and think about what you are going to say next. It will come out with more clarity and confidence.

Gestures

Gestures are great fun to incorporate into your speaking and presenting. When your hands move, so does your voice. Gestures are a way of underpinning vocal modulation.

When you write a report on paper, you might bold some words or underline phrases to create emphasis. Using a gesture is a lot like underlining a word or a concept. Try to have your gestures match what you're saying (i.e., don't use limp hands if you have a power message and don't use a pounding hand for a gentle message).

Assess how comfortable you are with gesturing and work to find movements that feel natural to you. Watch the activity and energy level of the person you're speaking with.

If they are high-energy and their hands are constantly moving, add some animation to your own message. If they are sitting perfectly still with their hands in their lap, tone down or stop your own hand movements.

There are two ways of thinking about gestures: one, gesturing for added interest and comprehension, and two, not gesturing. Find your rest positions.

When you're rehearsing your presentation, think about where a gesture might enhance a moment, add energy, or clarify a point. It's always good to practice these in advance. That being said, you don't want to be gesturing the whole time because then you might just look frenzied or nervous. Too many gestures can be distracting.

First, practice standing still. What happens to your hands? Do they drop listlessly at your sides? I suggest placing your hands mid-body, around waist height. You don't want to drop your hands low and clasp them. We call this the fig leaf position, because your hands mimic the fig leaves that artists used to place on the private parts of statues for modesty's sake. You don't want your audience thinking about your private parts.

If you keep your hands at waist height, try clasping them palm to palm or resting your fingertips together. Practice in front of a mirror or a friend to determine what pose looks most natural on you. You can also rest your hands on the edge of flip charts, or you can hold a clicker end to end with both hands. The idea is to give your hands a place to go when they are not gesturing but also finding a position that allows you to resume gesturing easily.

You can rest your hand lightly on a chair or a table if you're in a conference in a room. Take your time, and practice a variety of movements in rehearsal so that when you speak, they look natural and spontaneous.

Posture

I've been talking about posture a lot more in the era of Zoom presenting than I used to. Most people were raised with a parent who said, "Stand up straight!"

We all should have listened.

Posture is an indication of your willingness to be there. It also creates an impression of confidence when you stand tall and look ready for work.

I've seen a lot of Zoom slouching and sloppy chair positions. You can be too casual.

I talk a great deal to my clients about how to make an entrance. The beginnings of meetings matter. We'll go over their power introductions, and then I'll ask, "Have you thought about how you're entering the room for the meeting?"

You don't make a grand entrance when on Zoom, but you do give off impressions. Sit up tall and ready, and make great eye contact with your screen's camera. Even if you don't like to see yourself on screen, get into the habit of taking an initial glance to see if your posture is good.

Movement

Similar to posture, movement is something that I encourage my clients to think about more than they currently do. Your presentation starts the moment you enter a room, perhaps even a few steps before you get to the door. How you enter the room can signal: I want to be here. I'm ready to do business. I'm engaged and delighted to see you. I have executive presence.

We've all seen people come rushing into rooms hunched over, carrying pads of paper and rushing to the conference table to throw their items on the table. Then they sit down quickly as if they just ran a race and there was a time limit on how long they could spend getting from door to table. This kind of movement signals "junior."

Contrast that with someone who comes in, pauses just over the threshold to make eye contact, and greets the people in the room before sauntering over to the table. This kind of movement signals "senior."

I would encourage you to consider your entrance and adjust how you sit at the table. Take a moment to straighten your shoulders and pull your head up. Display your confidence and your own sense of importance in your movement.

Language

A few words on language (pun intended). We talked above about how to handle speaking in a second or third language, but, in general, it's important to try to remove jargon from your presentations and meetings. It's very easy to get caught up and use commonly repeated company slogans and sayings. Audiences can often hear what I call "jargon fatigue" in those phrases that have been said one hundred times.

Work to put the concept into your own words because, if you continually quote someone else's language, the phrase will lose all resonance. Audiences are smart. They don't need fancy words to realize you're intelligent and charming. Keep your language simple and conversational.

Dress

As I write this today, the dress code in business in corporate America has undergone a significant change post-COVID-19. Gone are the suits and ties that were the everyday expectation in many workplaces.

Most businesses have adopted a more casual style. But there are still challenges for both men and women in the workplace in finding the right attire.

It's a good habit to inquire about a dress code when visiting a client or prospect. (Remember to ask a follow-up question. There's a big difference between "suburb casual" and "big city casual.")

Internally, observe what the senior people in your firm wear and emulate them in a position-appropriate manner. In other words, dress aspirationally but not too much higher than your current pay grade.

One of my private equity clients was based in New York. He traveled the country to meet with clients. He tended to wear his tailored suits with his gold Rolex on his wrist and gold pen in his shirt pocket. When I suggested he should remove the watch and pen before going to meet with a group of union workers, he was offended. "This is how I dress, Cathy."

I asked him to consider what message he might be inadvertently giving to the group he was going to meet. A New York banker decked out in expensive clothes coming to negotiate with them was perhaps creating too wide a divide. We talked about how a slight moderation of his style might be more respectful to his audience. It's not necessary for you to imitate your audience so much as it is to understand their context. Dress code is an important aspect of creating rapport.

On the flipside of the above story, you might also learn that they have an expectation of what they want you to look like. A banker once told me a story about visiting his Greek shipping clients. He noticed that they were always in casual attire with deck shoes. One day, for his usual visit, he walked in wearing casual attire and deck shoes. He told me he'll never forget the look of displeasure on his client's face. It turned out that his client liked the fact that his banker showed up dressed to the nines, when he, the shipowner, was in casual attire and deck shoes. My client said he never made that mistake again!

So, you can see there's lots of nuance, which is why it's important to ask questions, observe your client's style, and think carefully before walking into any room.

Honesty matters, too. Many years ago, when I was taking over a new region, a colleague was giving me the lowdown on an employee I would soon be managing, who used to report to this colleague. Let's call the employee Sally.

He said, "You know, Sally would be great if she ever went beyond her goals."

I asked him, "Is she meeting her goals?" and he told me that she was. "But she never goes beyond." I said, "Did you tell her that you expected her to produce beyond her goals?"

He said, "No, I didn't think I had to. She should have just known."

Then he leaned in to whisper, "You know, there is one more thing about Sally."

"What is it?" I asked.

"She dresses immodestly." (He used another term.)

"Oh, my goodness!" I said. "What did she say when you told her?"

He looked appalled and said, "I could never tell her that …"

So, this poor woman was meeting her goals and maybe not dressing quite right for the job, but no one had given her any feedback.

The very first time I met her, I sat her down and said, "I have two very important things to tell you. One, when I give you a goal, try to come in 10 percent—or more—higher than the goal. And two, I'd like you to go out and buy one black suit and one blue suit. Buy lower heels. Pull your hair back and get a plain shirt. Dress like that every time you come in for the monthly meeting with senior management. In addition, I want you to stand up at every meeting and make one or two comments per meeting. Can you promise me you'll do that?"

She said, " Absolutely."

One year later, when I was promoting her, people asked, "What did you do to make Sally so successful?" I said, "I didn't do anything. She was always terrific. She just needed to dress the part."

11

EFFECTIVE MEETINGS

"Great things are not done by impulse, but by a series of small things brought together."

—VINCENT VAN GOGH

The two most nerve-racking parts of any meeting or presentation are the beginning and the end. These are the times that "all eyes are on you," and most people feel a rush of self-consciousness and nerves.

Rehearse these bookends, and you'll have two strong moments to anchor the rest.

A quick rubric for starting a meeting is to use the following format:

- Who?
- What?
- Why?
- How?
- Outcome.

Imagine you're conducting an internal meeting. You have a project to deliver and a timeline that must be adhered to. You've brought together the people who will make it happen.

Who is in the room? Introduce the people and parties. Make no assumptions! Better to introduce people to each other twice than never clarify who is in the room. What are you all there to accomplish? This sounds so obvious, but often we forget to say it clearly at the outset.

Why is this goal important and worth everyone's time? It is helpful to remember the greater goals at play and why a project will advance the firm's reputation or make workstreams more productive.

How will the meeting unfold? For example: "We'll start with a quick update and then offer suggestions for what the next steps will be. We want this to be interactive but with targeted efforts."

What is the hoped-for outcome of this meeting? "We expect to leave this room having agreed on next steps and their priority order." If you say this out loud, you will have a higher likelihood of achieving the goal!

This hip-pocket outline will help you kick off your meetings with simplicity and command.

Now let's look at some ways to improve our external meetings.

Focus on the client.

Most of my clients go to meetings with their clients with an idea of what they want to accomplish (remember our objective setting from chapter 2).

I like to think about the "music" in the meeting, the balance of soprano and treble, bass and alto. The judicious use of rests or pauses. What is the balance of talking? Is enough time being given to the client or prospect to voice their thoughts and not just their questions?

Focus on the interactions.

There will often be some attendees who dominate a meeting just by their comfort and SOCIAL STYLE®, responding verbally and quickly to every point that is made. This can often prevent the slower-paced, quieter communicators from interacting. You can use a combination of eye contact, pausing, and even gesturing to invite the quieter participants to engage. I often react to the facial expressions of attendees with something like, "I see your brow has furrowed; is that a question?" Or, "It looks as if what was just said resonates with you. Would you like to talk further about it?"

Once, in a meeting I was running, a man rolled his eyes right after I'd made a statement. I stopped and said, "Wow, that was a strong reaction. Can you tell me what it was I said that made you roll your eyes?" He laughed and said, "I was actually reacting to an email I just saw on my phone. It had nothing to do with what you just said!" Everyone laughed, and it dispelled my interpretation (and perhaps that of others in the room) that he was actively disagreeing with me.

Focus on the team.

Most of my global clients have a company value of working well together, and they call it something like their one-team approach. There is talk of sharing information for the benefit of the client relationship—stories of harmonious communications between team members and of better deals being completed.

This is a critical and powerful approach. Unfortunately, everyone claims to do it—and better than their peers. So, who to believe?

Here are some thoughts to make the message actually connect better:

1. Rehearse your introductions so no one presenter goes on too long. Make sure you listen to each other with attention (and possible delight!).

2. Avoid using catchphrases or acronyms: "The OTA is our biggest differentiator." (*I intentionally inserted the overused differentiator word here!*) Use your own language to describe how it happens and what it feels like to work in this manner. It will be more credible. If you must use the firm's catchphrase descriptor, preface it with "We like to call it ...," which will offer your client a glimpse into the company jargon.
3. Don't overstate the love you have for your colleagues. Rather, show it in respectful behaviors as you share the stage/message.
4. Describe what your colleague(s) did in the exchange of information that was out of the ordinary: "You wouldn't naturally assume that this called for a ______, but she had a hunch that this other team might see it differently."
5. Talk about the ways the firm supports and rewards the out-of-the-box connections. Share initiatives or everyday ways that connection is encouraged.
6. Offer the financial results as a mark of success, but don't forget to highlight the roles of trust and creativity in getting there.
7. Be careful how you compare this practice to competitors' practices. If you have a firsthand frame of reference, such as "I worked at the competitor for five years before coming here ..." you can establish credibility. Without that, tread lightly.
8. Be mindful that it's OK to say that you work together as a team, but it will be seen as a lie if you don't operate as

a seamless unit while speaking with the client. Uplifting a colleague also raises the perception of your collegiality.

9. Model the collaborative behaviors by asking insightful questions and/or leading a brainstorming moment with the prospect to show your inclination to listen to all ideas.
10. Be specific in citing the benefits, answering what the collaborative approach means to them—for example, "The whole firm is working for you, we can get deals done faster, and you'll get insights into global trends and markets."

Keep in mind that this "one team" approach will resonate more with some clients than with others. If you've started the meeting by getting the prospect or client to talk first, maybe even telling you how they wish to work with a new partner, there's a chance they'll talk about their own collaborative philosophy. What a beautiful way to link their values to yours!

Focus on the close.

I call this "putting the bow on the package."

In any presentation, the conclusion is just as important as the introduction—if not more so. It's the moment when you have the audience's attention and are poised to leave them with a lasting impression. This is where you make your final impact and guide them toward the next steps.

Too many meetings end with a splutter and a hasty, "Are there any more questions?" If you've used a good structure to organize your message, you should have a powerful conclusion right at hand. Practicing this in advance is a way to ensure that you boldly ask for the business, investment, feedback, or the next meeting.

Having crafted your objective of what you want this audience to think, do, or feel, you can design a closing statement in line with those goals.

You can ask for their business, you can secure the next meeting, or you agree to an interim exchange of information. You can even ask them how they are feeling—in that moment—about partnering with you. It's a wonderful (if slightly daring) way to repair any misconceptions or information gaps before you leave the room.

This is your last impression of the day. Best to make it count.

Balance in Meetings

As we've discussed, I like to think of the ebb and flow of a meeting being like a musical score. You wouldn't want a piece of music that plays only one instrument on one note for an hour. Yet, in a lot of meetings, one side of the table tends to dominate because they are *presenting*. This is why a focus on conversing is key—it reminds you that you want to hear your audience's voice responding to what you are saying.

We'll talk about increasing the amount of time you listen as one way help to with this balance. The best way to stop a run-on sentence or presentation is simply to stop talking: to pause.

Remember, in the thinking time that the pause allows, your audience has a window to hear what you just said, and they have a chance to interject. You have a window to watch how they are reacting to the information (nonverbal responses), and you have the chance to change direction, if needed.

Making a meeting rehearsal a mandatory step in your premeeting preparation is always a power play. It only takes a few minutes to decide who the leader of the meeting will be. This is not always so obvious. You may have two to three people of equal seniority attending a high-stakes meeting. Any one of the senior people would be comfortable taking charge and driving the agenda, but if no one decides which one of the leaders will play that role, then there can be inadvertent competition for airtime and control.

Drafting an agenda and designating who owns which part of the meeting helps make it seamless when you're in the room. It eliminates the need to ask permission to speak (from your colleagues!), and it helps everyone listen more attentively because they're not wasting energy on looking for opportunities to insert their voice.

Another aspect that can be negotiated before the meeting begins is agreement on how best to interrupt each other. We've established that there is generally at least one person on every team who likes to go on and on. The question may be answered, the rapport may be achieved, but this person keeps on talking. You might agree that whoever notices this happening (regardless of seniority or title) has permission to say, "Andy, your passion is showing! It may be time for us to wrap up."

I was in a meeting last month in which the client across the table was clearly happy with the outcome and felt there was no more to say. He didn't articulate this; he was simply displaying it nonverbally: a glance at the clock, a speeding up of his pace, and a movement in the chair as if to stand up. We have a long-term business relationship, so our rapport is easy and there's a lot of trust between us. Therefore, since we'd had a productive chat and a good outcome, I did not take offense at any of these displays. I simply closed my laptop and said, "This was great. Thank you so much. Why don't we end here and use these extra minutes to get ready for our respective next meetings?"

His face lit up, and he said, "That's much appreciated." He hustled out the door.

I've never known a person or a team that was upset when a meeting ended early. Departing gracefully once your message has landed is another method of honoring the time constraints of your audience.

Encouraging Participation and Managing Quiet Participants

I am often brought in to help junior team members speak up in meetings. The leaders of the firm want their junior talent to be empowered and share their opinions. Often, they forget how very hard it is to break into a meeting that is being run by senior officers.

A well-meaning senior leader might try to remedy this by turning to a junior member of the team and asking, "What do you think about that?" in the middle of the meeting. A welcome invitation, yet it might be an uncomfortable moment for the junior team member. First, there's the attention aspect: All eyes turning on an individual creates a surge of energy and self-consciousness—this discomfort can be magnified if the moment wasn't anticipated. Second, there's the message aspect: The junior will want to give the perfect response, earning the respect of their senior colleague and the esteem of the client. That's a lot to take in and respond to in a few seconds.

But imagine if the senior officer pulled the junior team member aside before the meeting and said, "I'd like you to have a voice in this meeting today. Once we finish discussing the opportunities in the market, I would like to pass the baton to you with a question. A good response at that time will be to emphasize the timing of the opportunity …"

In that way, when the question comes, the less-seasoned member of the team is expecting it and knows that the answer has already been vetted as appropriate and necessary.

A side benefit: The ease with which the exchange happens will showcase how well the team works together.

Conversational Intelligence

By now you've probably figured out that we should stop making presentations and instead engage in what I call "heightened" conversations. By this, I mean that we should use a conversational tone but rehearse the content so it comes out clearly and engagingly. On a practical level, this means using a natural tone of voice and everyday semantics. Again, lose the business jargon and the slightly fake "presenter voice." It is so much more engaging for the audience to be "in conversation" with you than to feel as if they're attending a college lecture.

As it turns out, there's much more to having a conversation than many of us know: There's neuroscience underpinning what happens during conversations. In their *Psychology Today* article, "The Neuroscience of Conversations," Niklas Balboa and Richard Glaser offer so many insights. Among them, the following ideas really resonated with me.

Conversational intelligence is known as C-IQ. When we engage in these conversations, we trigger the brain and set our mood, our ability to feel safe, and even our ability to look forward and anticipate the future. In the process, the brain responds physically and emotionally and starts to create hormones and neurotransmitters that either make us feel safe and trusting or fearful and anxious.

Clearly, we want to evoke the "feel-good" conversational style. When this happens, the brain will produce higher levels of dopamine, oxytocin, endorphins, and other biochemicals to create a sense of well-being.

There are three kinds of conversations:

Level I: Transactional conversations: These involve asking and telling, confirming what we know and giving and receiving information.

Level II: Positional conversations: These involve advocating and inquiring, defending what we know and expressing strong opinions.

Level III: Transformational conversations: These are cocreated events involving sharing and discovering. These kinds of conversations lead to more innovation, insight, and connection.

Our brains are wired to detect either trust or distrust in conversations. When our conversations trigger a safe space, we increase our ability to think strategically, improve our foresight, and empathize more effectively.

The practice of conversing *with* your audience members, rather than presenting *to* them, could be the basis of a long-term, trusted business relationship.

Handling Conflicts or Disagreements

But even in the best of those trusted relationships, conflicts and disagreements can occur in the course of decision-making. There are many ways to navigate these moments effectively.

First, try to ascertain the root of the conflict. Is there a value that's been ignored or trampled on? Is there a perceived slight, such as not acknowledging someone's rank and authority?

Second, observe how the conflict is manifesting. Is the other person shouting? Pounding the table? Or verbally saying, "You are wrong"?

When you're trying to reduce tension, think about coming in at an energy level that is just underneath that of the other person. If you need to raise your voice, keep it one degree lower than theirs when you respond. Lower your tone further with the very next thing you say and continue in that manner. The descending volume will help diffuse the intensity of the discussion. It's very important at the outset, though, that your volume is a near match. That helps the other person know and feel that you understand the strength of their reaction.

This method can work in the opposite scenario as well. If someone is disagreeing but speaking in a very low voice with low energy, you don't want to come in with an aggressively high tone, saying, "Perk up; we can solve this!" That would serve to separate you further. It's better to come in with a tone of voice and energy that is just above them, then slowly escalate your volume and energy sentence by sentence. This will help elevate the mood, energy, and momentum.

Managing Virtual or Hybrid Meetings

The techniques I've talked about above are great when you're meeting in person, but what about those ubiquitous Zoom or virtual meetings? It's a bit more difficult to achieve engagement and manage energy when you're just looking at boxes on a screen, but it's worth any extra effort.

Rules of engagement: I start most of my group Zooms with some comments on the rules of engagement. I tell them it's a courtesy to me, as the speaker or facilitator, for them to put their cameras on so I can react to their faces. Then I give them permission to interrupt me without ceremony: "Just unmute yourself and say, Cathy, I have a question. Then identify yourself by name so I can visually find your face on the screen." It doesn't work to wait politely to be acknowledged because there are so many other distractions.

When I lead large groups, I prefer to have a colleague join me, as I mentioned before, to watch the chat and the Zoom room while I'm speaking. I offer the participants the option of writing comments in the chat for those who are uncomfortable interjecting. Also, if my companion sees a facial reaction or a raised hand, she will just speak up and interrupt me to bring my attention to that individual.

Virtual Conversation Circle

The other technique I recommend is to not spend all of the virtual meeting time sharing a PowerPoint presentation and talking to the screen. As often as I can, I stop the sharing and return to the group room where I can see twenty-four faces on each screen. I call this the virtual conversation circle. The individual boxes get larger, I can see more of the group reaction to what's being said, and it invites people to speak about what we just learned.

Pausing becomes even more critical in virtual meetings. When you, as a leader of a meeting, stop talking and patiently wait, your participants will have time to unmute and make a comment. These pauses are longer than the ones you use for in-person meetings; it takes an extra moment for people to realize that you are not going to say something.

Follow-Ups

All good meetings come to an end. After your powerful closing remarks and gracious departure, there is still a connection to maintain.

You've likely reviewed the agreed next steps as part of your exit comments. Hopefully, you've asked the question, "What is your preferred method for follow-up? Email, telephone, or text?" You might even ask their preferred cadence. Do they want to hear from you in a week or two?

Take your client or prospect's preferred SOCIAL STYLE into account.

Will they want a detailed list or timeline of dates and to-do items? Will they want a casual telephone call and anecdotal check-in?

Whatever your next steps are, honor whatever has been promised. You are demonstrating the attentiveness and care that will be the hallmark of your professional relationship.

12

ANNUAL MEETINGS

"An executive is someone who can tell a story and make people believe it."

—JACK WELCH

I spend many weeks of the year in auditoriums, sitting in the audience watching my clients get up on stage to deliver their annual general meeting presentations. This is the mandatory meeting during which the company or firm must share its business results with its investors. The annual meeting also provides the investors with the opportunity to meet the minds behind the magic, the upcoming talent, the steady performers, and the new visionaries. It is a way of affirming the investors' continued trust and confidence that the firm and its members are good stewards of their capital.

There is usually a theme or call to action for every meeting, and a long list of speakers who have each been given three to five minutes to encapsulate twelve months' worth of performance. Consider it the firm's highlight reel of the year.

For those of you who have attended these meetings or presented at these meetings, you know they usually entail a lineup of presentations, panel discussions, and videotaped messages from firm leaders or dignitaries. Almost every speaker is given just a few minutes to persuade the audience that the deal flow is fine and the leadership efforts are on point.

Often, the entire event has a theme, and the individual speakers spend many, many hours of preparation time deciding what to say and getting approval for their message from both management and compliance. PowerPoint slides are drawn up, reviewed, and revised endlessly.

I recommend you start thinking about the delivery of the message far earlier, and even before the slides are completed.

When my clients arrive for their first coaching session, often it's without any idea of what their conclusion is going to be. It seems natural to let the story unfold and then decide what the takeaway message will be.

I like to start with the end in mind. So, one of my first questions will be, "What's the last thing you are going to say?"

Then, "What is the big idea you want me to grasp?"

When the speaker articulates the final sentence or two, even in a rough manner, it immediately starts to clarify the rest of the presentation. In order to land "here," one must cover this point or that case study, but perhaps there's no need to elaborate on extraneous details.

In previous chapters, we talked about the fear of public speaking and also the gifts we can glean from actors. The annual meeting is the place where both of those realities collide.

One of my early clients was the head of a private equity group. He was handsome, brilliant, and very successful. He was also confident and fully convinced that the audience wanted to hear his every thought. In other words, he would often run over his allotted thirty-minute segment. One year, he talked for a full hour beyond this designated time. There was no denying that what he was saying was substantive, but it was exhaustive and exhausting.

Our capacity to listen and our attention spans have diminished. When he finally concluded, there was a quick, mad dash by everyone in the audience for the doors (and the restrooms).

This experience is not unique. In fact, research on attention span reveals that the average person's ability to focus on a single task has dramatically decreased over the years, largely due to the rise of digital devices and constant notifications. According to a study by Microsoft in 2015, the average human attention span has dropped to just eight seconds, shorter than that of a goldfish, which is around nine seconds (Microsoft, 2015).[20] This dramatic decline has important implications for how we structure and deliver presentations. What once might have been an acceptable length of time for a deep dive into complex subjects is now seen as overwhelming.

In the age of information overload, we need to rethink how we present information. Instead of aiming to fill a specific time slot with an exhaustive list of facts, we need to focus on delivering clear, concise, and engaging messages that respect the audience's limited attention span. A successful presentation is not about how much information we can deliver but how effectively we can capture and maintain the audience's attention, making the information memorable and actionable.

No one at our private equity client's firm had the heart to tell him he was being too long-winded. When I gave him the feedback, he was a little skeptical but willing to try to work on reducing his content.

Over the years of working with him, he found a way to deliver the same high degree of quality in terms of knowledge and insight in a much more engaging and time-sensitive manner. His limited partners would tease him about getting his own TV talk show because he was

---

20 Kevin McSpadden, "You Now Have a Shorter Attention Span Than a Goldfish," *Time Magazine*, May 14, 2015, time.com/3858309/attention-spans-goldfish.

so entertaining and at ease in front of the room. They were enjoying him—and his messages—more.

This is because he remembered that everyone in that room was listening to him independently, one at a time. It's easy to think of a large audience as a single entity, but it is not. It is made up of individuals, each deciding whether to engage with a speaker or not.

And that's a key takeaway for anyone: The audience is listening to you one person at a time. We don't need to check in with our neighbor to ask whether they believe what the speaker is saying. Each person has a singular way of interpreting the world. So, when you're the speaker, you are talking to individuals, not one massive body of humanity.

Therefore, you must look these individuals in the eye and let them know they are seen. In a large room, you accomplish this by breaking the room into geographic sections or groupings. Perhaps you cluster three tables together—observe if people are gathered at dining tables—or three rows, if you're in an auditorium. You look at an individual in the cluster (say the woman with the green blouse) and make eye contact with her. Because of the distance from the stage to that location, the entire cluster may feel that you are looking directly at them. This technique not only makes each person feel noticed; it also ensures that your delivery is more personable and engaging. Perhaps you've had this experience at a concert before.

So, by focusing on early rehearsal and crisping up the message, speakers can develop and refine their communication skills, actively listen to their colleagues, land a powerful message, and create an engaging experience. Armed with these newfound abilities, our clients can connect with their audiences on a deeper level, leave a lasting impact, and maybe, just maybe, enjoy themselves while ensuring that their annual meetings become truly unforgettable.

Then it's time for a dress rehearsal. As I've said before, this is a priority, not a luxury. The dress rehearsal is, in my opinion, the key to a successful annual meeting. Yet, this practice is the last thing that anyone seems to want to do.

I'm a big advocate of putting "practice time" or even "thinking time" on the calendar. We don't do that enough. There's a lot of resistance to practicing, in general. And in business. Rampant perfectionism? Probably. When you talk about practicing in sports, theater, or music, everyone recognizes the importance of hitting the wrong notes in the dry run.

Dress rehearsals are clunky. Speakers may be walking on the venue stage for the first time and finding that the lights are so bright they can't see their audience. Often, they realize that their notes, carefully placed into the confidence monitor (the screens at the foot of the stage that show you your slides), are not particularly helpful. You can't read a paragraph, in tiny letters, from six feet away. I see a lot of presenters with their heads bowed, as if in reverence, to the confidence monitors as they try to discern a word or a nugget that will help.

I say, "fewer words, bigger font." The idea is to keep your narrative moving, not to try to read aloud to a crowd.

The dress rehearsal often reveals what was done well or poorly in the preparation. If a speaker has worked with their slides, transitions, and main concepts enough to know the story through line, the dress rehearsal will be about putting the finishing touches on the delivery: the walking and talking on stage. If a speaker hasn't worked with their message enough, they will leave a dress rehearsal and spend the next several hours going over the speech again and again. I recognize that sometimes this is dictated by a lack of time—work always takes precedence over rehearsal. I am just suggesting fighting harder for those pre-meeting minutes to rehearse.

Once at a dress rehearsal, it's important to focus on the technical aspects so they don't distract during the main event. Are the slides projected right behind you on stage, or off to the side? Can you refer to them while speaking? Do you need to move to one side of the stage or the other so people can see your visual aids? Can you navigate the stage with ease? Are your shoes comfortable? Are there obstacles on the stage (brackets, tape, wires, rugs, etc.) that can trip you up? Does the microphone battery fit easily in a pocket, or do you need a belt to attach it to? Where are the audience seats situated? Can you see everybody while you're speaking? Answering these types of questions and walking a stage will result in a more natural use of the space, a more conversational delivery, and a lot more connection with the audience.

Again, there's some mess in the dress rehearsal. That's the way it's supposed to be. In theater lore, a bad dress rehearsal means you'll have a great performance. It's always worth the pain.

Ask Me Anything: Some Thoughts on Panel Presenting

Panel discussions are a staple of annual meetings, and of my clients' public interactions. All too often, most of the prep time is used to craft carefully worded questions and responses. I recommend you focus, instead, on what the *experience* will be for your guest panelists and your audience.

First of all, as is often repeated, the more natural, slightly flawed, very human presenters are the most engaging. When presenters know their material enough to comment on how they feel about the findings or the results, then we are in conversation with them and we trust them more.

When a group of supersmart business leaders sits down for a panel discussion, the last thing you want to hear is a list of overly curated questions being answered in a rehearsed and message-laden method. You want to see the true reactions and interactions of these minds that are running the business. There's an energy that happens when they jump in to respond to a fellow panelist's comment or observation.

At one annual meeting, my favorite moment was when the moderator, the senior-most executive on the panel, said, "I'm not going to ask you the questions we prepared …" and threw the question sheet over his shoulder. The whole audience laughed and leaned forward to see what was going to happen next.

What happened next was a great conversation among senior leaders who teased each other and offered insights in equal measure, all in a relaxed manner. It was the most enjoyable segment of the day.

What's more important than a perfect answer? Balance. Give a balanced answer about the positives and negatives of your topic. Also, balance the talking time so that everyone on the panel gets about the same amount of speaking time. The moderator is supposed to keep an eye on this, but it's also great when one colleague turns to another and says, "Do you agree?" or "What's your view?"

Think about the implications for a firm that is known for its collaboration culture—you can *show* your partners how it manifests rather than just *telling* them.

A mixture of panel discussions and traditional slide presentations breaks up the outpouring of information and creates more entertainment value. You don't need as many visual aids when people are just talking or telling stories; you're engaged by their style and thought.

When you are managing the Q&A session, you may not have prepared for the specific questions asked; that makes answering with confidence all the more important. Whether you are engaged in panel discussions or direct audience feedback, the same rules apply: Be authentic and confident. This is your opportunity to further engage with your audience and address concerns. When you start by establishing ground rules, you let the audience know when and how to ask questions, whether they should hold them until the end or ask as you go along. Always remain calm and composed, no matter what questions come your way. (Easier said than done!) When you respond, take a moment to listen fully before you answer; this will give you time to gather your thoughts and ensure your answer is as relevant as possible.

It's also important to ask clarifying questions if you're unsure about what's being asked. This will give you time to think, and it shows the audience that you are engaged and genuinely interested in addressing their concerns. If a question stumps you, you will want to pause, gather your thoughts, or even admit that you do not have the answer. Be authentic and thoughtful in your responses, which will make you seem more credible and trustworthy.

Things to Consider for Panel Discussions

Keep the questions short. I see a lot of airtime taken up by someone who is refining a question. More often than not, it becomes a leading question with a foregone conclusion.

1. *Agree on key messages* you'd like to land, but don't over-rehearse them.
2. *Invite fewer people* to the panel so there is ample time for everyone to opine.

3. *Remember to talk to the audience.* Too often, the panel members talk to each other or to the moderator. Interact with the audience.
4. *Bring the passion.* As the subject matter expert, add some color to why you've stayed with the strategy/work for so long.
5. *Let the jewel shine.* If you've invited a dignitary or special guest, remember that they are the jewel and you are the prongs that put them in the best light.
6. *Have some fun.* It is wonderful to see people who work together enjoy working together.
7. *Nail the conclusion.* This is something that can be given some framing before the panel has even begun. Articulate the reason the panel was created in the first place!

13

ELEMENTS OF ENGAGEMENT

"A picture is worth a thousand words."

—FREDERICK R. BARNARD

What are visual aids?

When I said "visual aid" before, what did you think of? The first thing that most of my clients think of is the PowerPoint deck. I don't know who the first person was to bring a PowerPoint presentation to a meeting, but I'll bet they had no idea that this style of presentation would become so pervasive and overused.

It's remarkable, really, how many words can be squeezed onto a single page! Not admirable—or even useful—just remarkable.

Think for a moment of your favorite storybook when you were a child. I'll bet you can see the cover of that book in your mind's eye, and you may even have a clear memory of a beautifully illustrated page. It may have been calming or scary, primary or pastel, but it most certainly made you feel a certain way. It made the story memorable. It probably helped you imagine the character's feelings.

Do you remember the font of the words on the page?

I'd be surprised if you did.

A visual aid should be something that helps your listener engage with the story. It should also be something that helps you, as the storyteller, stay on track.

Think of the last PowerPoint deck you read. Did it give you a thrill? It's OK to say yes, because maybe a particular revenue chart got your heart pumping. But in my experience, they are pretty dull missives.

Our brains are primarily visual processors. The brain can process images sixty thousand times faster than text.[21] Visual images get more easily encoded into long-term memory. They evoke emotions and can create more engagement.

Interacting with Visual Aids

Scripts, decks, notes, and other visual aids are wonderful support systems for you as the speaker. How you interact with them can make or break your seamless interaction with the audience.

Imagine you are seated around a table with a group of individuals. You each have a PowerPoint deck on the table in front of you. As you present from the deck, all heads are bowed as the individuals read from the page. There's a good chance your head will be bowed, too.

What a lost opportunity for connection! How much harder it will be to spotlight you and your firm's talents!

The trick is to use your eye contact techniques to glance at the page or your notes, then lift your eyes to look directly at someone across the table. It doesn't matter if they are not looking back. When you add your vocal projection and send it in their direction, they will sense your eyes on them, hear the voice directed at them, and lift their heads to meet you.

---

21 Studies find visuals improve learning by 400 percent and "increas[e] 'human bandwidth'—the capacity to take in, comprehend, and more efficiently synthesize large amounts of new information." Research by 3M recognized the astonishing speed at which the brain processes visuals. Andrew Herkert, "How Visuals Help You Remember Information," TruScribe, January 30, 2020, truscribe.com/blog/how-visuals-help-you-remember-information.

You may have heard the phrase *one thought to one person.* This means that it's best to give a discreet thought to one listener and then move on to the next listener. If you don't make an effort to engage with everyone in the room, you might end up talking to one person for a larger percentage of time. This might be OK if the person you are speaking with is the boss or the decision-maker, but it's important you do this with intention.

If you find yourself presenting in a larger forum and you have slides projected on a screen behind you, it's important not to turn and speak to the slides. That will send all your energy (vocal, visual, and physical) back to the screen instead of out to the audience.

The trick is to use a gesture, such as a raised arm and hand, to indicate a section of the larger page, then turn your head and eyes back to the audience before you speak. At Rogen International, we were taught to "touch, turn, and talk." Touch the visual aid with your eye contact, turn to the audience, and then talk.

Microphones

Microphones are wonderful to use when you are in a large auditorium or conference center. Common types of equipment are handheld microphones and lavaliers, the kind that clip to your blouse or jacket and have a small battery pack. Using a handheld microphone can be fun if you are comfortable holding something the entire time you are speaking. It is important to hold it close to your mouth to get the best vocal resonance.

Listening

When people seek out communications coaching, they almost always want to improve their executive presence, their impact, their messaging, and their clarity. We rarely have someone come to us who says, "My primary goal is to become a better listener." But as renowned author Maya Angelou once said, "The single most important element in communication is the ability to listen."

So much of being a master communicator is about being able to receive information, by listening and by observing. Heightening these skills will yield huge rewards.

Robert Bolton, the author of *People Skills* and a proponent of the SOCIAL STYLE® construct, talks about listening in three clusters: attending, following, and reflecting.

Bolton's Three Skills

Attending is a way of nonverbally communicating that you sense the importance of what the speaker is saying and that you're committed to trying your best to understand them. Practice attending by assuming a relaxed-but-alert posture of involvement, in which you face the speaker squarely, leaning forward just slightly. Keep your arms and legs uncrossed to avoid communicating defensiveness, and maintain an appropriate distance of about three feet.

Following is about staying out of the speaker's way so you can find out how they view the situation. This means paying attention to nonverbal cues that suggest they have something on their mind, as well as sending noncoercive invitations to talk, or door openers:

"Tell me more," "I see," "Really?" and "What's on your mind?"

Reflective listening is when you exhibit the following listening skills: paraphrasing, reflecting feelings, reflecting meaning, and summative reflection. *Paraphrasing* is when the listener relays the essence of the speaker's content in their own words. A paraphrase is concise, cuts through the clutter, and focuses on the speaker's central message.

Reflecting feelings, on the other hand, is when the listener relays the emotional crux of the speaker's message. The speaker may be experiencing a lot of emotions, but as they talk, the listener tries to determine the principal one.

These are wonderful ways to gauge how you might be currently listening to someone. It seems easy, but what gets in the way of our hearing what is being said? There are four fundamental obstacles:

- **Physical:** You are not comfortable. This could mean anything from having eaten something that doesn't agree with you to simply sitting with the sun in your eyes.
- **Mental:** When you think about what you're going to say next, or reflect on what you've just said, this prevents you from hearing what's being said now.
- **Emotional:** You may be disagreeing with something that was said a moment ago, and as you make the mental argument against that point, you miss what is being spoken in the moment.
- **Time:** We are always trying to squeeze oversized messages into thirty- or sixty-minute slots, and as we hurry to make a timely exit, we may stop listening to whomever is speaking.

Levels of Listening

A helpful practice is to think about how you are listening.

Are you **listening without interest**? You may be engaged in small talk and not have any interest in what is being shared. This is not optimal, but it is polite.

Or perhaps you're **listening to confirm**. You may be paying attention to any language or discourse that supports your point of view on a matter, project, or recommendation. This is not necessarily a bad way to listen, but it does make you vulnerable to missing other important clues.

You might simply be **listening for specifics**, such as when the client will have the funds to invest or what their preferred timeline is. This is useful for moving deals and business forward, but when listening for specifics, you might ignore or miss information that doesn't seem immediately relevant to you but might be important in the long-term relationship.

Finally, you may **listen to learn**. While this sounds ideal, because listening that turns into learning is a wonderful activity, it does have a downside. Listening to learn takes quite a long time because you will be directing the course of the conversation far less.

I suggest to my clients that they choose a portion of each meeting to sit back and just listen to learn. In that way, they can keep a small time limitation on the activity while they train themselves to be patient and just let information flow.

Remove the barriers to listening that you can. Turn off your phone. Change your sun-drenched seat. Eat a healthier lunch. Shorten your messages to fit into fewer minutes. Jot down the ideas that challenge you and come back to them later.

Catch yourself listening and try to assess how you are listening. Are you trying to confirm something or learn something new? Vary the ways you listen in each meeting. The bottom line is this: Listening is as important as speaking when you are making a connection or furthering a business relationship.

Questioning

Most of my clients tell me that they are very curious and great at asking questions. I find that most of them can improve on their probing skills. First, we have to fight the natural instinct to ask closed-ended questions: What is your budget? When do you want to implement the strategy? Where is the meeting?

Are you? Is that? May I? Will you? Can I? Should we? Have you? Could you? Is it? Did you?

These may give you specific answers, but you will learn very little about the individual you are speaking with that day. They are likely to respond with one- or two-word answers.

If you use open-ended questions, they are more likely to give you a robust answer, especially if you've established rapport with them.

What are? How? What is? Why? In what way? Why do you think? Can you elaborate?

Any question that gets the other person to give a longer answer gives you an opportunity to gain more insight. I recently asked a group that I was facilitating to see if they could ask questions to determine my newest hobby. People started shouting out questions:

"What is your hobby?" (I declined to answer that one!)

"What do you do on weekends?"

"How long do you spend on this hobby?"

"Are you doing it alone or with other people?"

I was generous in my answers, so they figured out pretty quickly that I was taking some kind of language class.

I stopped them for a moment and said, "You're getting close to the answer, but what have you learned about me?"

They had gotten so focused on finding the answer to my question that they forgot there was a person standing before them whom they could learn about (especially if I were a potential future partner).

They opened up their questions:

"Why are you learning another language?"

"Why is that significant to you?"

And they soon uncovered that I was learning Korean in order to take one of my sons, who was born in Korea, back to the country of his birth. They also learned that we were hoping this might allow us to meet his birth mother, and that, even if we couldn't do that, it would allow him to learn more about his culture and wonderful heritage.

It was an important reminder that there is artistry in how you combine open and closed questions to move a conversation along, get information, and learn the values of the person you are speaking with.

What? Which? Why?

When you are asking questions, start out broad: What are the areas of greatest interest to you (about our firm, our product, or our team)? Which of these is most important to you? Why? You will then have a focused list of areas of interest and the highest-priority item, as well as the reason underpinning its importance.

A simple return to the original list with the questions, "Which is the next most important to you?" and "Why?" will further confirm the priority order of issues to be addressed.

In that way, you are speaking your audience's language and addressing their most pressing issues in priority order, thereby demonstrating that you are a partner who listens, learns, and pays attention.

Two Down, One Along

Another simple but powerful technique is remembering to ask two questions "down" before moving on to another series of questions. What do I mean by that? Imagine you ask someone, "Why are you looking to buy a house in this neighborhood?" You may be asking this as the seller, trying to tee up a great listing of all the neighborhood amenities.

If the answer is, "I've always wanted to live in a neighborhood like this," you might be eager to jump in right away with that convincing list of perks and advantages. If, instead, you pause and ask two more questions on that one response, you might gain much more important information.

You might ask, "Was your neighborhood growing up so very different?" and then after that, "What does being in a neighborhood like this mean to you?" You will then be speaking in the language of values. You might be talking about affluence or family security or access to the arts. Even if the neighborhood in question holds all of those benefits, you may need to speak only about the one that is most resonant with the buyer.

Guiding Values

I remember how much the concept of listening for values resonated for me when I first heard it put that way. Think of the last conversation you had or the last business meeting you attended. Were you listening to confirm details, learn a procedure, or figure out the next steps to be taken? Ask yourself, "How much time did I spend trying to listen for the communication that pointed me toward the values of the people in the room?"

That is the treasure you're digging for when you are communicating: What are the values that rule their worldview, and how can we find the commonality in what we both hold to be true? How can we build a business relationship that satisfies both of our core value systems?

A person's guiding values come from a combination of experience values and current imposed values. The **experience values** are those beliefs we gain from the life we have lived. We may learn some of them from our family, friends, and colleagues. As the name suggests, we have learned them over time and experienced them having an effect on our worldview.

There are other values that are imposed on us by society or our corporations. If your firm has a dress code, that is a **current imposed value.** It's a value you have to abide by until the time you leave the company.

Why is learning someone's values so important? People make decisions based on their values. As J. P. Morgan said, "A man always has two reasons for doing anything: a good reason and the real reason."

The good reason is based on rational values, need, and criteria. The real reason is more often based on his emotional, political, and cultural values. What does he want?

14

AUTHENTICITY

"The ability to show vulnerability is a sign of strength, not weakness. True courage is being willing to be open and honest about who you are."

—SHERYL SANDBERG

I remember when authenticity had just started to be the buzzword in seemingly all the business articles. The leadership experts were urging people to be authentic at work. It may seem odd now because it's so much a part of our work dialogue, but there was a time before authenticity was considered a desirable goal. In fact, I was so indoctrinated that my first reaction was, "Oh, no, no—it's not safe for everyone to be authentic at work." I'd had too many conversations with clients about their carefully crafted work personas. Most of us were still trying to be our best, perfect selves.

This was the era when banks had a strict set of current imposed values. It was made very clear that I was expected to wear a dress or a skirt, not pants, to the office. My outfit should include a blazer. My heels should be clean and polished, but not too high, and stockings were mandatory. Many of us were trying to mimic the look of men's suits to show our equal influence and power. To that end, women wore tiny silk scarves as neck ties to bring attention to our heads and brains. Hair was to be pulled back and neat.

This was not how I dressed on the weekends. So, just by the metric of costume, I was being someone else at work. It made me think of my acting days. Janet used to teach me, "You have to authentically feel something; you can't just act an emotion. That's how you connect with your audience."

So, was my work self an inauthentic version of me, or just another facet of me? Was there a way to merge the two?

Of course, my work self was authentic. As I've gotten older and survived mistakes, misfires, and successes, it now makes sense to me. Being authentic is about giving yourself permission to be flawed—to show up and try, whether or not you succeed. Brené Brown famously said, "To be authentic, we must cultivate the courage to be imperfect—and vulnerable."

When my husband, John, and I were living in New York, we had a small apartment on the Upper West Side. It was technically a two-bedroom, but the second room was very tiny, so we designated it our home office. In essence, it was a paper closet because it was filled with papers, books, and files. We closed the door whenever we had people over.

The living room was a good size, but we had filled it with a large sectional couch, a TV and stand, storage cabinets, and a round coffee table. We had lots of pictures on the walls, and we had books piled everywhere (my fault). The windowsill was covered with potted plants. It was cozy, but cluttered.

We had a couple over for dinner, and we passed a very pleasant evening. The next day, I saw the woman, who had been our guest, at work. She thanked me for the evening and said, "I expected your home to be different." She was trying to be polite, but I sensed that what she meant was "I expected it to be better." I pressed her to explain what it was she had expected. She said, "You are so polished at work. I thought your house was going to be pristine and museum-like, but it was very comfortable." She laughed and went on to say that she liked me better knowing that my home wasn't perfect.

I was startled by this revelation. It took me a beat to get over my own disappointment that the apartment hadn't lived up to her high expectations. The second thought was, *How could she not know that I was inherently relaxed and comfortable?* It made me think about how I was showing up at work. That's also when I came to my oft-stated conclusion that people don't like perfect people. We find them to be distant from us and our lifestyle. They make us either jealous or uncomfortable.

Is Changing Your Style Inauthentic?

People often tell me that when they try to flex to a different SOCIAL STYLE, they feel as if they're being inauthentic. I suggest that's because they're trying to mimic someone instead of finding their own unique way to manifest the style.

It takes awareness and practice, including some trial and error, to find your method of modifying your own way of communicating to meet someone where they are. When you do, it becomes just one more skill and another way of being authentically you.

One note of caution about authenticity: This permission to be authentic is still not applicable everywhere, even after all these years. People are still overcome by fear of judgment and the desire to keep up appearances. There continue to be toxic work environments in which employees don't have trust or psychological safety. Hierarchies and rigid thinking still erode trust and transparency and make it hard for people to feel safe.

Can authenticity be taken too far? Yes, if someone defines it as the right to say whatever they think, no matter how hurtful.

It's important not to define authenticity as a license to be rude or insensitive to others. It's about being honest and respectful. It's not about perfection; it's about connection.

Good leaders know that connection is what underpins motivation and inspiration.

Throughout this book, I've talked about how to use skills to tighten messages and increase their power, as well as how to use your hands, eyes, body, and voice to enliven your stories and create your corporate image. I've introduced a structure to line up your thoughts and deliver them coherently. All of these techniques and/or processes combine to give you choices in how to create and deliver a message or request. The versatility to make that message resonate across the SOCIAL STYLE matrix is how you start to inspire someone.

When people think about leadership, they often imagine someone standing in front of a crowd, crying, "Follow me!" and inspiring everyone to action. At the heart of leadership, though, is the ability to forge relationships and trust. Great leaders know that inspiring someone is an individual act; it happens one person at a time before it grows into a group experience.

You will appreciate my bias, but authentic, honest communication is the cornerstone of great leadership. Leaders create meaningful connections by sharing their victories and defeats, not by pretending to be all-powerful and always right. In a culture in which open discourse and acceptance of all ideas are fostered, more ideas get airtime and more feedback is given. More ideas mean more good ideas. More feedback means more growth. Through transparency and integrity, a leader creates psychological safety for the whole team.

How does that translate into impact? A leader who has an empowered, trusting team will see a higher volume of ideas and better ideas. If the people on a team know that their leader trusts them, they will take action and be more empowered; they won't be constantly seeking permission.

The concept is simple, but the ability to show up every day, greatness and all, flaws and all, requires courage. It helps to be able to look in a mirror, give yourself feedback, and laugh.

Getting good at this requires, first, a sense of direction: What kind of leader are you becoming? Then, know your audience: Who are you trying to inspire? What is your line in the sand?

What Does It Take to Be Authentic?

It takes courage to be seen as you are and to stand—flawed—in front of others.

It takes insight into what made you the way you are, what motivates you, and it takes patience to gain these insights for the people you work with and hope to inspire.

It means knowing your weaknesses. In that way, you can build a team of people with complementary talents and stop expecting that you can be everything to everyone.

I've talked a lot about flaws, but it's equally important to be able to celebrate your own strengths. Many of you will be hesitant to do this, thinking it might be unseemly or conceited, but it's truly just about getting an accurate assessment of the powers/tools you have to work with.

The most authentic leaders are also able to receive feedback without getting overly defensive, or overly wounded. The ability to say, "Yes, I did that and I own that" roots you in honesty and credibility.

On the other hand, authentic leaders know how and when to give feedback. They focus on the feedback that will elevate the recipient, give them an honest appraisal, and keep their sense of self and pride intact.

At the heart of good leadership is the same recipe that is at the heart of good communication: Know who you are dealing with and what they need from you.

Authentic leaders should also foster a touch of defiance to keep the parts of themselves that are different from the norm.

How Do Leaders Turn These Traits into Alignment?

First, they work hard to cultivate excellent communication. Everyone around them knows what the greater goal is and can clearly see their role in achieving it.

Leaders should also work to hold their teams accountable through feedback, as mentioned above, but also through rewards for great ideation and effort. Not all rewards are monetary.

Some people want acknowledgement, some people want a title, some people want a challenge, some people want free rein, and some people want a feeling of accomplishment. Others are motivated by pride and appreciation.

When leaders align people's individual values with those of the organization or team, they create buy-in and understanding. When people's values are being met, they often begin to feel passionate about the work at hand.

Lest this sound as if everyone should be holding hands and singing *Kumbaya*, it's important for authentic leaders to foster a culture that encourages positive dissent and disagreement. Being able to say no to power or think again often creates the best refinements and improvements.

So, Where to Start?

As you grow in your leadership, start with serious self-reflection. What has caused you to be successful so far? What has consistently gotten in your way? Are these traits immutable or changeable?

Accept what you can't change. Can you find ways to work around the deficiency? Maybe you can devise a new system or leverage the talents of others on the team.

Take the time to own what is true and strong and uniquely you. Be prepared to share that with everyone.

Do some exploring to understand how others already view you. What did you do to inspire someone? What did you do to offend someone? Were the outcomes in your control?

When you've done your self-reflection and augmented it with some information from the field, prepare to share your understanding of yourself with those you work with so they can help you brainstorm the best systems and procedures for all involved. It's important that you stay as close to reality as you can. Avoid describing your fantasy self; stay rooted in the present, no matter how scary that might be.

So, to end where we began, take some time to make your leadership communications as true as they can be. Start with the clarity of your message. Simple words, simple direction, and clear purpose.

Help everyone see where the goal is located and the possible paths to that goal. Get everyone moving in the same direction. Inspire them by speaking to the values you share and the values that will be enhanced by success.

Make sure you're always using your words, not just parroting someone else's message. A message doesn't need to be perfect; it needs to be real and sound like you.

Remember to keep the emotion in the message. If you don't have feelings about what you're trying to accomplish, it will be hard to get anyone else interested in it.

Above all, be honest. Being a leader means you may have to concede a point or take a loss. It takes bravery to talk about the goals that scare you or the disappointment in an outcome. Equally, be honest about the pride you feel when you collectively get it right.

Finally, remember to be consistent. Leaders should repeat their key goals, values, and commitments often. The more people hear a version of the same story, the more they can trust in you and your beliefs.

In order to make an authentic impact as a leader, be committed to following your own values, being transparent in how you're doing so, and creating an environment for everyone around you to feel informed, safe, and inspired.

Continuous Improvement

I've tried to share with you the simple, magical ways in which you can improve your leadership communication skills. There's a caveat, though. There really isn't a magic wand that will make this all come together overnight. You must practice, practice, practice.

The work of being an authentic leader happens before you start to lead. It's knowing who you are, what your gifts are, and what you need to augment and nurture to become the leader your team needs. It's no wonder that communication is the underpinning of how you share this with the world.

The way to communication mastery is through rehearsing as much as you can. It's at rehearsal that you make the mistakes, tweak the message, and better your abilities. It's the same thing with leadership.

It's at rehearsal that you try a different way of saying something or a different pace. When you rehearse with a team member or colleague, you gain each other's trust and an understanding of the likely cadence of their delivery. If you set a direction for the team and it doesn't work, the ability to own it and redirect is a critical step in your future success and growth as a leader.

Core to growth is incorporating the practice of debriefing and delivering feedback. It's hard to give constructive feedback; we often feel uncomfortable that we are judging someone else. But if we don't give honest feedback, then there's no chance of improvement. We should give ourselves performance reviews as well.

I recommend stepping out of a meeting and doing a quick round of "Here's what we did well," followed by "Here's what we can do better *next time*." Most of you will want to jump right in with the critique, but it's very important that you identify what you did brilliantly, too, and not take it for granted. You'll want to trust that it will be repeatable.

Max Landsberg introduced the AID (action, impact, do) model of feedback in his book *The Tao of Coaching*.

Here's how you use it:

1. You describe the **action**.
2. You explain the **impact** of that action.
3. You suggest what you want them to **do** next time.

For example, you might say:

"Jack, when you introduced yourself at the outset, your energy was great, but the length of the introduction was too long.

"The impact of the long introduction was that you lost the interest of our decision-maker. He almost rolled his eyes!

"Before the next meeting, let's rehearse the introduction together. In that way, we'll have it buttoned up for the client."

CONCLUSION

MASTERING COMMUNICATION THROUGH CHALLENGE AND GROWTH

"It's not about perfection; it's about connection."

—CATHY C. BONCZEK

"Think of great communication as art. You start with a vision and acquire great tools (canvas, brushes, and paint). You determine the palette or color of the piece, then you start to paint. You may do many sketches or studies before you get the composition you envisioned. Most importantly, you just paint. With passion, patience, and perseverance, you can create a masterpiece."—Cathy C. Bonczek

I started the month of June 2023 with a terrible fall on a pickleball court. I managed to break both my arms. I was hospitalized, had surgery on both of my upper arms, spent some time in a rehab facility, and finally returned home. These were not the plans I'd had for my summer!

As I look back on my healing and reflect on what transpired, I had so many moments of communication gaps, near misses, and successes. At the time I was injured, I calmly told my friends they needed to call an ambulance and call my husband. Almost immediately, bystanders were yelling advice to me as I was face down on the court, unable to move because of my arms. They were admonishing me and trying to get me to sit up and get ready for the ambulance. Some even rolled me over onto my back—a serious break in injury protocol. It's lucky I didn't have a neck or spine injury! I was trying to say to them that I would wait to move until the medics got there, but it was hard to talk between spasms of pain.

People began squeezing my arms to determine if they thought I'd broken them. Let me just say, this was not pleasant. They were asking me, "What happened?" I finally said, "I am going to stop talking now. I am managing pain." I shut my eyes and my lips and let them discuss among themselves.

The club representatives were in a frenzy to gather my personal information. I had to ask one woman twice to seek out my husband, who, I assured her, would spell Bonczek for her. As I was being lifted into the ambulance, I told her to please stop asking me where I lived.

Next, it was hard to communicate to people what I was feeling. The medics in the ambulance wanted to know which arm hurt more. I said they both felt pretty awful. I didn't feel as if they believed me until the x-rays came back. The breaks were so bad that technicians stopped by my emergency room cubby just to see me and the x-rays because word spread quickly about the freak accident.

By that point, I was very uncomfortable but not suffering acute pain due to medication. Yet I still needed to be alert for the communication of diagnosis and possible remediation, i.e., surgery or casts.

We were advised that surgery was called for, due to the severity of the breaks. We wouldn't know if it would be one arm or two until the doctor arrived for the surgery and made a determination.

The next decision was, Who should we have do the surgery? The best in the hospital for special surgery or the doctor who happened to be on call that evening? A seemingly obvious answer, but having the renowned doctor do it meant that I would have to wait several days until he returned to town: two and a half excruciating days for the assurance that I would heal faster having been in expert surgical hands.

The next communications were about all the limitations and restrictions that I was now subject to during rehab. I kept trying to tell the doctors and nurses that these restrictions weren't resonating with me. I couldn't fathom doing nothing for weeks on end. No travel, no swimming, and no lifting of anything heavier than a teacup. No summer.

Additionally, there was a conversation with a psychologist to see whether I needed sessions to ward off depression, but he deemed me an exceedingly positive injured person.

Even communicating with myself was tricky. I actively told myself, *You are not going to let this get you down.* But, why did I think this had happened? What was the lesson I was supposed to walk away with? I thought it was about letting things go, recognizing when you have no control over circumstances, but that's something I'll explore later.

At the end of the day, I walked away grateful for a random comment. My oncologist stopped by the hospital after my surgery. He said, "Cathy, if your arms hadn't taken the brunt of this fall, your head would have. You might not be here." *Suddenly, the story was completely different.* I wasn't the victim of a horrible, stupid mistake meted out by fate; I was the person lucky enough to survive a bad fall and walk away with just two broken arms.

I share this as a vivid reminder to keep asking, "How can you change your current story to serve you better?"

As we reach the final pages of this journey, I want to leave you with a thought: Communication is the heartbeat of leadership. It's not just about the words you speak or the messages you deliver. It's about how you connect, how you engage, and how you listen.

Every conversation, every presentation, every meeting is an opportunity to frame the experience and make a lasting impact. Whether you're leading a team, delivering a keynote, or having a one-on-one conversation, your ability to communicate with clarity, confidence, and authenticity will shape your success.

Now it's time to put what you've learned into action. Take the steps to strengthen your communication.

Listen actively and be fully present in each conversation. Don't just wait to speak; understand, absorb, and reflect.

Engage with authenticity and do not be afraid to be vulnerable; share your true self and connect on a deeper level.

Own your presence, whether on stage or in a meeting; the way you carry yourself communicates volumes. Stand tall, speak with clarity, and lead with confidence.

Use storytelling to inspire, to persuade, and to share your vision.

Embrace feedback because communication is a two-way street. Seek feedback to grow and improve your skills.

You have everything within you to be a master communicator. It's not a talent reserved for a few; it's a skill you can develop every single day. Practice, reflect, and continue to refine your voice.

As you embark on your communication journey, remember this: Strong communicators aren't born; they are made. And the steps you take today will shape the leader you become tomorrow.

So, go out there and make your voice heard. Lead with purpose, speak with passion, and listen with intent. Your words have the power to change the world.

I have worked with hundreds of talented clients at all stages of their careers. It has been my great delight to see them develop their skills and become great orators, partners, colleagues, and leaders.

The magic is in the simplicity of the techniques and the diligence you bring to working with them.

I hope that you will enjoy these ideas, tools, and suggestions and that they bolster your success!

ABOUT THE AUTHOR

Coach Cathy specializes in working with senior executives, domestically and internationally, to hone their high-stakes communications, client pitches, and leadership delivery skills. She has more than twenty-five years of professional and consulting experience and expertise. She likes to say she puts the Clarity, Conciseness, and Business focus into CCB.

Her experience as a communications coach includes training and consulting with global asset managers, private equity firms, hedge fund managers, and investment banks in the areas of leadership communication, fundraising launches, IPO (initial public offering) presentations, annual and investor meetings, industry conferences and panels, presentation skills and mastery, virtual impact, influence skills, relationship selling, negotiation skills, earnings calls, elevator pitches, and deal/pitch consulting.

Before creating CCB Communications, Coach Cathy was a managing partner with Rogen International. Her responsibilities there included being a member of the North American management team, driving new business development, leading the banking and finance team, running the company's largest worldwide account, and spearheading a global team that developed a proprietary professional development program.

She started her career as a Suez Canal transit specialist for Worms Permal Shipping, later choosing to become a banking executive. She won several awards for sales performance and leadership at Marine Midland Bank, Chemical Bank, Bank of Boston, and NatWest Bank.

A graduate of Cornell University, she is currently an alumni class officer. She is a former member of the Advisory Board for The Moment Institute for Narrative Coaching and Integrative Development.

Cathy studied acting with Janet Sarno, the Ensemble Studio Theater, and the Brooklyn Heights Players. She studied voice with Linda Eckard and Denise Esposito. She studies writing with Drew Lamm. She is conversant in French, having attended Université Sorbonne Nouvelle in Paris, and is learning to speak Korean.